T3-BVC-588

Aspects of Harmony in Schoenberg's Six Little Piano Pieces, Op. 19

Aspects of Harmony in Schoenberg's Six Little Piano Pieces, Op. 19

by Kenneth L. Hicken

Associate Professor of Music
The University of Lethbridge
Lethbridge, Alberta, Canada, T1K 3M4

Frye Publishing
Winnipeg, Canada

Cover design by June Lucyk-Ricklefs
Book design by Betty Schroeder-Roberts
Inside art by Sophi Hicken

Copyright 1984 by Frye Publishing
Suite 104, 1565 Willson Place
Winnipeg, Manitoba, Canada R3T 4H1

ISBN: 0-919741-42-8

Printed and bound in Canada

Contents

Preface

This monograph represents a recently completed study in which I have arrived at an answer to the following question: How can the harmonic organization of Schoenberg's *Six Little Piano Pieces,* Op. 19 be understood if, as a premise, this composer's atonal language be regarded as an outgrowth of the traditional Western musical language? This answer, which constitutes *a* way of understanding this organization (in my opinion, a valid and musically viable way), consists of results which have been obtained primarily via my own personal study of the music as seen on the printed score, as heard when played at the piano, and as conceptualized in terms of the above-mentioned premise.

Background

In 1962, Merrill Bradshaw reported his discovery in early works of Webern of a type of simultaneous merging of harmonies from two different keys.[1] In 1968 or 1969, in my own study of the "Introduction"[2,3] and "Theme"[4] of Schoenberg's *Variations for Orchestra*, Op. 31, I discovered a somewhat analogous type of harmonic organization and postulated that this type was based upon an underlying principle which I termed "fused bitonality." As orginally conceived, this principle—which I viewed as a sophisticated extension of the principle of tonality—stipulated (1) organization of pitch into two intimately intertwined "tonal components," (2) organization of pitch within each component in keeping with a modest extension of traditional tonal practice, (3) orientation of one component about one tonal center and orientation of the other component about a second, simultaneous tonal center, and (4) separation of these centers by the interval of a tritone. Thinking that fused bitonality might perhaps be the most fundamental principle of pitch organization in Schoenberg's twelve-tone works (as is tonality in 18th and 19th Century compositions), I subsequently sought and found what I regarded as evidence of fused-bitonal organization in a modest but wide-ranging selection of samples from other serial works of his, and, in 1974, presented a paper dealing with such organization, at the first International Schoenberg Congress, in Vienna.[5]

Later, in an attempt to see if the harmonic workings of entire compositions could be explained in a musically meaningful fashion with reference to fused bitonality, I concentrated upon the following three works: (1) the *Six Little Piano Pieces*, Op. 19, from the composer's pre-serial atonal period, (2) *De Profundis*, Op. 50B, his final twelve-tone composition to be completed, and (3) the *Suite for Piano*, Op. 25, his first multi-movement serial

Schoenberg self-portrait, 1910

[1] Merrill K. Bradshaw, "Tonal Organization in the Early Works of Anton Webern" (D.M.A. thesis, University of Illinois, 1962).

[2] Kenneth L. Hicken, "Structure and Prolongation: Tonal and Serial Organization in the 'Introduction' of Schoenberg's *Variations for Orchestra*" (Ph.D. dissertation, Brigham Young University, 1970).

[3] Hicken, "Structure and Prolongation: Tonal and Serial Organization in the 'Introduction' of Schoenberg's *Variations for Orchestra*" (summary of author's Ph.D. dissertation), *Musicological Annual*, 10 (1974), pp. 27-47.

[4] Hicken, "Schoenberg's 'Atonality': Fused bitonality?" *Tempo*, 109 (June 1974), pp. 27-36.

[5] Hicken, "Towards a Theory of Harmony in Schoenberg's Twelve-Tone Music," in *Bericht über den 1. Kongress der Internationalen Schönberg-Gesellschaft* (Vienna: Elisabeth Lafite, 1978), pp. 87-97.

work. In 1978 fused-bitonal analyses of Op. 19 and Op. 50B were finished, and early in 1979 examination of Op. 25 was well underway.

Yet while the explanations of harmony in Op. 19 and Op. 50B looked perfectly plausible on paper, something was wrong. As I learned to play the Op. 19 pieces at the piano and became better acquainted with their sound, it became increasingly clear that many passages in this work, although often highly chromatic, nevertheless sounded as if they were "mono-tonal," i.e., in solely one key at a time. Accordingly, for these passages no need existed for an explanation via fused bitonality. Continuing aural and conceptual involvement with these pieces eventually led me to realize that the harmonic organization of almost all of this composition could be viably explained in an aurally defensible fashion, in terms of outgrowth from the traditional language, but without any recourse to fused bitonality whatsoever.[6] Further such involvement convinced me that the harmonic organization of the entire work could be so explained. Such an explanation is what is offered in this monograph.

[6] Hicken, "Tonal Organization in Schoenberg's *Six Little Piano Pieces*, Op. 19," *Canadian University Music Review*, 1 (1980), pp. 130-146.

Acknowledgements

Of those who have contributed directly or indirectly to this study, particularly the following deserve a sincere expression of gratitude: (1) my friend and colleague at the University of Lethbridge, Professor Dean G. Blair of the Department of Music, whose consideration and discussion with me from time to time of my analyses of Op. 19, of concepts and details involved therein, and of the written text itself, as all of these have evolved, have been most helpful; (2) the Department's secretary, Sheila Harrison, for cheerful and conscientious work in typing the manuscript in its various stages; (3) my wife, Alice, for unending patience and for her insistence that the study had to be completed, even if other matters had to wait; and (4) our children, who, while not always understanding why "Dad's book" should take so long, have looked forward without complaint to the time when it would be finished.

All quotations for the *Six Little Piano Pieces*, Op. 19, are used by permission of Belmont Music Publishers, Los Angeles, California 90049 and Universal Edition, Vienna.

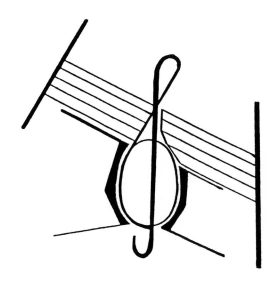

I *Introduction and Overview*

Problem and Approach

Deciphering Schoenberg's atonal harmony, particularly in a musically comprehensible fashion capable of dealing with the music's sound as well as its appearance on paper, has long been one of this century's most obstinate musical challenges. Not only is the problem difficult; it is significant, so much so as to be central to an understanding of two of the most influential musical concepts of our time, atonality and serialism, as applied by their principal pioneer and as adopted or adapted by successive composers.

Solution of this problem, a monumental achievement, would greatly facilitate: (1) comprehension of Schoenberg's atonal language as such; (2) performance of his atonal and serial music in a more knowledgeable manner; and (3) determination of a presumed correlation between harmony and serialism in his 12-tone works. It should also provide a basis for assessing the extent to which successive atonal composers have continued on in his language as opposed to having merely avoided traditional tonal relationships.

Approaches towards a solution vary of course. If Schoenberg's atonality is regarded as being totally divorced from traditional major-minor tonality, then any attempt to solve the problem must naturally exclude consideration of the materials, principles, and procedures of eighteenth- and nineteenth-century harmony. On the other hand, if (in view of *Gurrelieder* and *Verklärte Nacht*, the *Harmonielehre*, his own teaching based upon music of traditional masters, his acknowledged indebtedness to them as his principal teachers,[1] and his own persistent "longing to return to the older style"[2]) his atonal language be regarded as an outgrowth of the established tonal language, and is thus rooted therein, then an approach open to finding traditional harmonic elements, vestigial or otherwise, in his atonal harmony is very much in order. Such is the approach taken in the present study of the *Six Little Piano Pieces*, Op. 19.

---

[1] Arnold Schoenberg, "National Music (2)," in *Style and Idea*, ed. by Leonard Stein with trans. by Leo Black (New York: St. Martins Press, 1975), pp. 173-174.

[2] Schoenberg, "On revient toujours," in *Style and Idea*, p. 109.

Within the context of attempting to understand this harmony, analysis of these pieces is appropriate for two reasons. First, their chronological placement (1911) between *Erwartung* (1909) and *Pierrot Lunaire* (1912) suggests the probability that their language will be reasonably representative of at least that of the composer's pre-serial atonal writing. Second, their brevity makes comprehensive detailed harmonic analysis a feasible objective.

Findings

The findings of the study amply vindicate the approach taken. They show that while the harmonic aspect of Op. 19's language is characterized by the absence of certain features of traditional tonal organization, it is also characterized by an integration of (1) features retained intact from the tonal and modal systems and (2) modifications and extensions of features of these systems. These findings may be summarized as follows:

1. *Tonal Centers.* Pitch in Op. 19 is organized with reference to a succession of tonal centers, each note of the work being related to at least one center. However, the composition as a whole does not have a principal center, but is related rather to the succession itself.

2. *Modulation.* In all of the pieces but No. II, modulation occurs, generally via common chords. It takes place over all possible intervallic distances, i.e., from one through five semi-tones upwards and downwards, and the distance of a tritone upwards or downwards. Its frequency of occurrence varies greatly. The first and final centers of each modulating piece differ from each other, a feature suggesting the concept of progressive tonality. Similarly to the composition as a whole, no one of these five modulating pieces has its own principal tonal center.

3. *Overall Pattern of Tonal Centers.* In much the same way that the notes of a compound melody taken one at a time in succession imply two or more essentially concurrent melodic contours or lines, so this composition's tonal centers taken in turn suggest primarily a three-line texture. Accordingly, these centers, so taken, can be readily organized into a three-voice passage incorporating their suggested lines. This resultant passage, whose chordal structure and voice-leading comply by and large with nineteenth-century chromatic practice, modulates from G to E♭, concludes abruptly with no sense of harmonic finality, readily leads back to

its commencement harmony, and, with a slight adjustment in octave register, can repeat itself endlessly.

4. *Modal Orientation*. Organization of pitch occurs with reference, primarily, to major, minor, and Phrygian modes. One modal orientation can rapidly succeed another. Occasionally the orientation is bi-modal. Chromatic inflection within the context of a prevailing mode is often encountered.

5. *Consonance and Dissonance*. Although the overall level of dissonance in Op. 19 is much higher than in traditional tonal music, consonant intervals and chords do appear. Further, resolution of dissonant chords to consonant ones, while less frequent than movement from one dissonant chord to another, is not unusual. On the other hand, all phrases but two end with a dissonant chord.

6. *Voice Leading*. Of the two types of motion available to individual voices in chord-to-movement, conjunct and disjunct, the more fundamental type encountered in Op. 19 is the conjunct. This is so (1) because conjunct motion from members of one chord to members of another takes place very frequently in its own right and (2) because much of the disjunct motion from members of one chord to members of another would be conjunct if it were not for octave displacement.

7. *Harmonic Vocabulary*. Three basic classes of chord are found. In decreasing order of prevalence they are: "tertian," "dual-membered tertian," and "quartal." A hybrid type is termed "partially quartal." Non-harmonic tones also occur. As traditionally, chords here assume various forms. They may be solid, broken or partially broken, complete or incomplete, in root position or inverted, clearly stated or suggested, and in open or close position; they may occur in conjuction with one or more non-harmonic tones or with none.

8. *Tertian Chords*. These include most of the traditional array of triads, seventh chords, and ninths, as well as thirteenths and a far greater proportion of eleventh chords than is found in Western music of the eighteenth and nineteenth centuries. Other harmonic units are dyads (single thirds) and monads (single roots). The latter, although occurring rarely, and technically not chords, are included in this category because the kind of harmony which they as roots would generate most naturally is tertian.

9. *Dual-Membered Tertian Chords*. Each of these is such that at least one of its members (e.g., the third or fifth, etc.) is present in two forms (e.g., major *and* minor third, or perfect *and* diminished fifth, etc.). These chords range in size from thirteenths to dual-

membered counterparts of triads. Closely related to this class of harmony is a small group of "diminished-octave" chords, characterized by the presence of a diminished octave above the root.

10. *Quartal Chords.* Several quartal triads and tetrads and one quartal hexad occur. When considered from a traditional perspective, the tetrads and hexad can be readily explained as quartal arrangements of tertian eleventh chords, and each of the triads can be understood as a quartal arrangement of tertian elements, i.e., of tertian chord-members, or of tertian chord-members and a non-harmonic tone.

11. *Partially Quartal Chords.* A partially quartal chord is characterized by the occurrence of three or more but not all of its members in a quartal configuration. When considered from a traditional perspective as above, each of the several such chords encountered in this composition can be readily explained as a partially quartal arrangement of a tertain or a dual-membered tertian chord.

12. *Non-Harmonic Tones.* All of the standard non-harmonic tones occur. Occasionally octave displacement takes place in the approach to or departure from one of these.

13. *Tonal Functions.* Each tertian, dual-membered tertian, diminished-octave, and partially quartal chord has a root associated with a tonal function (tonic, dominant, mediant, etc.) or with a comparable function pertaining to a degree of a modal scale.

14. *Root Movement.* Most instances of movement from one chord to another involve a change of root. In these changes all possible intervallic distances are traversed, i.e., from one through five semitones upwards and downwards, and the distance of a tritone upwards or downwards. Root movement of a rising perfect fourth occurs most often, followed in order of decreasing frequency by movements of a falling perfect fourth, rising minor second and falling major third, and falling minor third.

15. *Root Shifts.* In some pivot chords, the root of the chord as approached differs from that of the chord as left. Such a change of root, occurring *within* a chordal structure rather than between a chord and its successor, is termed not a root "movement" but a root "shift."

16. *Root-Succession Patterns.* In much the same way that the notes of a compound melody taken one at a time in succession imply two or more concurrent melodic contours or lines, so the roots of each piece, taken in turn, suggest in most cases a three-

line texture, and can be arranged as a polyphonic passage incorporating these lines. The six passages so formed, in their chordal structure and voice-leading, also comply by and large with nineteenth-century chromatic practice. These passages, taken in sequential order, readily proceed from one to the next. Further, the passage derived from the roots of piece VI leads back to the one derived from the roots of piece I. Thus, like the succession of tonal centers, the succession of these passages can be repeated endlessly.

17. *Cadences.* Two of Op. 19's phrases end with an monad. The rest conclude in dissonant harmony. Half of the composition's phrases terminate with a tonic function, and a much smaller fraction do so with a dominant one. Nevertheless, not one instance of a straightforward traditional perfect authentic cadence, half cadence, or plagal cadence is found.

The foregoing assertions concerning the absence of certain traditional features and the retention, modification, or extension of others provide a conceptual introduction to the harmonic aspect of Op. 19's atonal mode of organization. Using this introduction as a basic frame of reference, specific detailed understanding of the composition's harmonic workings and of atonal organization *per se* as manifested therein may be acquired via study of analyses presented in chapters III and IV. As preparation for such study, familiarization with certain symbols, terms, concepts, and practices to be encountered, particularly in chapter III, is recommended. Accordingly, assistance towards this end is offered in the next chapter, "Symbols and Samples."

II Symbols and Samples

This study's primary exposition of Op. 19's harmonic organization is a set of six harmonic analyses—one for each piece— presented in chapter III. The prime purpose of the present chapter is to provide an introduction to these analyses, both to the symbolization used therein and to the musical organization which they reveal. Accordingly, relevant symbols, terms, concepts, and practices are explained, and musical examples are cited. This is done with reference to the following broad topics: (1) tonal centers and modal orientation; (2) chord symbols and chords (tertian, dual-membered tertian, diminished-octave tertian, partially quartal, and quartal); (3) modulation; and (4) chord-to-chord movement.

Tonal Centers and Modal Orientation

Tonal centers are designated by the first seven letters of the alphabet plus accidentals as needed. The major mode is indicated by capital letters, the minor mode by small-case ones, and church modes by capital letters with appended modal abbreviations (e.g., G means G major, b♭ means B♭ minor, and A♯_{Phr.} means A♯ Phrygian). When a passage's basic modal orientation is termed minor, reference to the harmonic form of the minor scale is implied. When a church-modal orientation is indicated, what is meant is simply that the designated mode with its particular pattern of intervals about a tonal center serves as a frame of reference. No retention of any Medieval or Renaissance subtleties regarding the mode or its usage is necessarily intended or suggested. Scale degrees of the Phrygian mode are given the same functional designations as scale degrees of the major and minor modes, i.e., tonic (first degree), supertonic (second degree), dominant (*fifth* degree), etc. This practice, any historical inconsistencies notwithstanding, is followed in the interest of uniform terminology.

Chord Symbols and Chords

1. *Tertian Chord Symbols.* Each tertian chord is identified with reference to: (1) the tonal center to which it is related; (2) the prevailing or least chromatic modal context (major, minor, ecclesiastical, or a possible combination); (3) its root; (4) the chord member farthest above the root (e.g., the seventh in a seventh chord, the ninth in a ninth chord, etc.); (5) the chord member in the bass; and (6) chord members chromatically altered from the diatonic form prescribed by the prevailing or least chromatic mode of reference. Monads are identified in terms of the first four of these items. With reference to items 3-6 and to certain other relevant matters, the following practice is observed:

a) Roots are identified by capital Roman numerals representing scale degrees (e.g., I, III, etc.).

6

b) The chord member farthest above the root is specified by an Arabic numeral at the right of the Roman numeral (e.g., VII^{11} refers to an eleventh chord on the leading tone, I^{3} to a third chord on the tonic, V^{1} to a monad on the dominant, etc.). For the sake of consistency, triads having a fifth as a chord member farthest above the root, are termed "fifth chords" (just as chords having a seventh as the chord member farthest above the root are termed "seventh chords"). Similarly, dyads, having only one interval, a third, above the root, are called "third chords."

c) The chord member in the bass is shown by an Arabic numeral placed below the Roman numeral (e.g., III^{7}_{7} refers to a mediant seventh chord having the seventh in the bass).

d) Chromatic alteration of chord members is shown by means of accidentals placed before the Arabic numerals referring to those members. A sharp indicates a rise of one semitone above the diatonic condition prescribed by the specified mode of reference, and a flat a lowering of one semitone (e.g., if VI^{9}_{5} were diatonic according to the mode of reference, then the ninth and third of $VI^{\flat 9}_{5 \sharp 3}$ would be one semitone lower and one semitone higher, respectively, than the ninth and third of the diatonic chord).

e) Locations in the score are specified with reference to pieces and to measure numbers, abbreviated "P." and "m." (plural = mm.), respectively. Measure numbers can include both complete and incomplete measures. Thus, P.III, m.6 refers to all or part of measure 6 in piece III.

f) In musical examples cited, when note spellings as determined by the harmonic analysis differ from note spellings in the score, then those of the analysis are used.

g) Stemless black noteheads enclosed in parentheses (e.g., (:)) refer to tones still sounding, or implied if no longer sounding. They may also refer to enharmonically equivalent respellings of preceding notes, as in the case of an enharmonically altered pivot chord.

h) Other abbreviations and their meanings include:

(1)	sug	—	suggested (e.g., sug V^{5})
(2)	imp	—	implied (e.g., imp I^{5})
(3)	a	—	added (e.g., a2 in $I^{5}_{a2 \atop 3}$ means an added 2nd in that chord)
(4)	Phr.	—	Phrygian (mode)
(5)	Loc.	—	Locrian (mode)
(6)	Mix.	—	Mixolydian (mode)

i) Non-harmonic tones without octave displacement are indicated by these abbreviations:

(1)	pt	—	passing tone
(2)	apt	—	altered passing tone
(3)	cpt	—	chromatic passing tone
(4)	nt	—	neighbor tone
(5)	apg	—	appoggiatura
(6)	uapg	—	unaccented appoggiatura
(7)	sn	—	suspension (tied or untied)
(8)	et	—	escape tone
(9)	an	—	anticipation
(10)	ped	—	pedal

The appoggiatura and escape tone occur both separately and within the context of the nota cambiata or changing tone figures (abbreviated "nc" and "ct," respectively).

The distinction intended between the passing tone, altered passing tone, and chromatic passing tone is clarified in example 1. There, in the melodic movement e♭'-d♮'-c♮', within the context of a C-minor tonic triad, d♮' is a passing tone; in the movement e♭'-d♭'-c♮', d♭' is an altered passing tone; in the movement e♭'-d♮'-d♭'-c♮', d♮' is a passing tone, and d♭' a chromatic passing tone.

Example 1

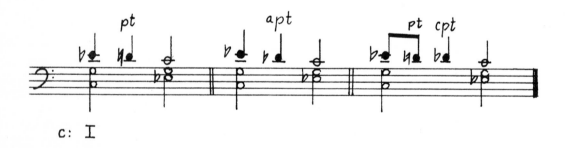

j) Non-harmonic tones with octave displacement, a much smaller group than those without it, are designated by the symbols for the latter, followed by a parenthesized "8" (e.g., pt(8), cpt(8), apg(8), etc.). Occassionally, an appoggiatura may also be understood as a different type of non-harmonic tone with octave displacement (e.g., P.I, m.1: apg = apt(8)). In such cases, if the octave-displaced tone is mentioned, its symbol will be enclosed in parentheses.

2. *Examples of Tertian Chords.* Four excerpts from the composition will now be cited, each of which contains at least three chords. All basic types of tertian chord from the dyad through the

thirteenth (also the monad) are represented, thereby providing a
reasonably comprehensive introduction to the work's tertian
harmonies and to symbols used to identify and describe them.

The first excerpt (example 2; from P.II, mm.2-4) shows
movement in G major involving the following harmonies, in the
order listed:

   a) a reiterated tonic major third chord (I^3);

   b) a partially broken fifth chord (I^5) having an implied root
and implied doubled third;

   c) a tonic eleventh chord ($I^{11}_{\#5}$) whose seventh, fifth, ninth,
and eleventh occur successively in the bass;

   d) another form of the eleventh chord, characterized by a
lowered ninth (see fig. 1);

   e) a major third chord on the tonic (I^3);

   f) a minor third chord on the subdominant ($IV^{\flat 3}$);

   g) the major third chord on the tonic (I^3).

The implied root ($g\natural^1$) and doubled third ($b\natural^1$) of the fifth
chord are notated by stemless black noteheads enclosed in
parentheses. The expressions 7→9 and 7→♭9 below the Roman
numerals of the eleventh chords signify movement in the bass
from the seventh of the initial chord to its diatonic ninth, and
movement from that seventh to the lowered ninth of the
subsequent chord, respectively. The $\#5$ indicates that the fifth of
both chords is a semitone higher than the diatonic fifth would be.
The ♭3 of the subdominant third chord means that the third is a
semitone lower than it would be diatonically in G major.

figure 1

$$\left(I^{11}_{\substack{\flat 9 \\ \#5}}\right)_{7\to\flat 9}$$

Example 2

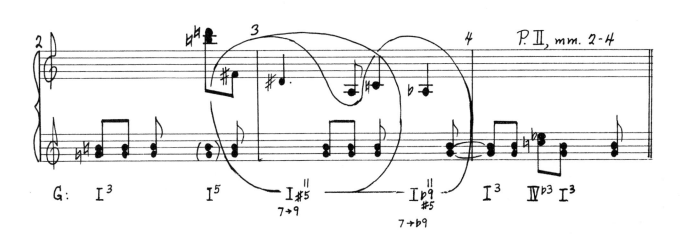

The next excerpt (example 3; from P.IV, mm.10-11) shows third and fifth chords in broken form, in B♭ minor. One of the fifth chords, on the subdominant, has its fifth as its lowest sounding member. This is indicated by a 5 placed beneath the Roman numeral (IV^5_5). The last of the third chords ($II^{\sharp 3}$) has a raised third, i.e., its third (e♮') is a semitone higher than its unaltered counterpart (e♭') in the harmonic form of the B♭-minor scale. (It will be recalled that when a passage's basic modal orientation is termed minor, reference to the harmonic form of the minor scale is implied. Thus, in such a context, any chromatic alterations are also specified with reference to that form as a standard.) This chord functions as a dominant of the dominant, which is symbolized in parentheses as follows: (V^3/V).

The final chord, a dominant triad ($V^5_{\flat 3}$), has a lowered third (a♭) as its lowest sounding member, i.e., a third one semitone lower than would be the case if it were an unaltered member of the harmonic form of the B♭-minor scale. The fifth of this chord (c♮') is implied from when it sounded as the root of $II^{\sharp 3}$. The fact that it is implied is represented by its enclosure in parentheses.

Example 3

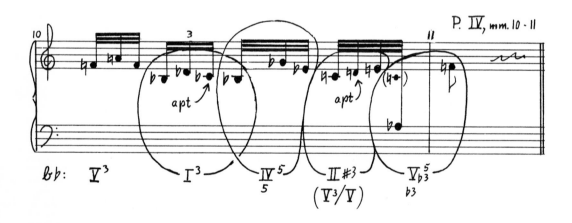

Two seventh chords, an Italian sixth, a chromatic eleventh chord, and a monad occur in the third excerpt illustrating tertian organization—all within the context of G major (example 4; from P.V., mm.9-11). The first seventh is a minor-major subdominant with lowered third in the bass ($IV^7_{\flat 3}$), this third (e♭) being a semitone below its diatonic counterpart (e♮) in the prevailing mode. The second chord is a root-position dominant seventh, embellished by an unaccented appoggiatura. The next chord, the

Italian sixth, is a fifth chord on the raised tonic, having a lowered third in the bass ($\text{I}^{5}_{\flat 3}$). This chord also functions as a secondary leading-tone chord of the supertonic ($\text{VII}^{5}_{\flat 3}/\text{II}$). It is attended by a chromatic passing tone in the treble voice ($c\sharp^{1}$). The eleventh chord is a supertonic ($\text{II}^{11}_{\sharp 7}$). Both its third ($c\sharp$) and seventh ($g\sharp$) are raised a semitone above their diatonic G-major counterparts. The final tone of the passage ($d\natural^{1}$) is a monad (V^{1}). It is a single root which represents a tonal function, the dominant, but which at the moment does not support or suggest any harmony. The $e\flat^{1}$ between the monad and the preceding eleventh chord serves as a neighbor.

Example 4

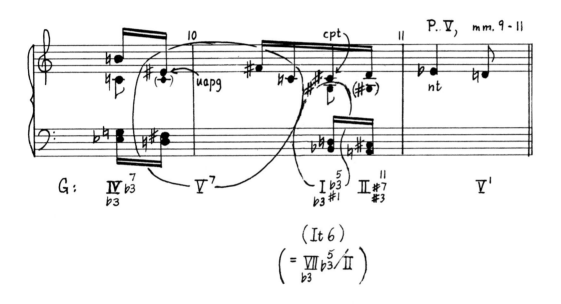

In the final excerpt illustrating tertian harmonies (example 5; from P.I, mm.5-6), two ninth chords and a thirteenth occur. Both ninth chords are inverted, the first ($\text{IV}^{9}_{\flat 3}$) having the seventh, and the second ($\text{IV}^{\flat 9}_{\sharp 3}$) having the ninth, in the bass. The first chord's root ($g\natural^{\prime\prime}$) occurs in the treble voice and is approached through a suspension.

Some overlapping takes place between the second ninth chord and the thirteenth chord which follows ($\text{III}^{13}_{\flat 7}$): the seventh ($d\natural^{\prime\prime\prime}$) and ninth ($f\natural^{\prime}$) of the former become the thirteenth and root, respectively, of the latter. Relative to the prevailing orientation of D major, the thirteenth chord's root and seventh have been lowered, as is indicated by the ♭1 and ♭7 of the chord symbol. However, in the D-Phrygian mode, this root and seventh would be diatonic (D: III^{13}). Thus, the chord may also be understood as a D-Phrygian mediant thirteenth occurring within a D-major context, as is to be inferred from the symbol's enclosure in parentheses. In other words, the chord may also be regarded as having been "borrowed" from the D-Phrygian mode.

Example 5

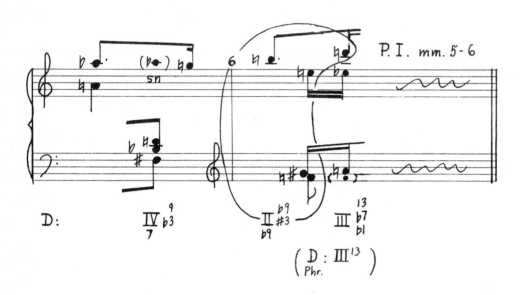

3. *Dual-Membered Tertian Chord Symbols.* Each dual-membered tertian chord differs from its tertian counterpart in only one respect, namely, in that at least one member of the former (e.g., the third or fifth, etc.) has two forms (e.g., minor *and* major thirds, or perfect *and* augmented fifths, etc.). Accordingly, all of the symbols explained with reference to tertian chords also apply here. Then, to specify the two forms of a dual member, the Arabic numeral referring to that member is placed twice at the right of the root-signifying Roman numeral, one instance above the other, each prefixed with the appropriate accidental. Thus, for example, in the case of a chord I$_{♮3 \atop ♭3}^{5}$ in the major mode, the dual member would be the third, and its two forms would be minor (indicated by ♭3) and major (indicated by ♮3). The ♮3 would specify a third which was diatonic in the prevailing mode; and the ♭3, one which was a semitone lower than its diatonic counterpart. In contrast, if the prevailing mode were Phrygian, then the same chord would be

12

written I$\overset{5}{\underset{\natural 3}{\sharp 3}}$. The $\natural$3 would still refer to a third which was diatonic in the prevailing mode, but now that third would be minor. The $\sharp$3, then, would specify a third a semitone higher than its diatonic counterpart, that is, a major one.

One type of dual-membered chord has dual "primes," the term "primes" being used in place of "roots" in keeping with the concept of one root per chord unless the chord is a polychord. The lower of these two primes, when they are adjacent, or if they were to be adjacent, i.e., an augmented prime apart, is regarded as the root (e.g., see fig. 2).

4. *Diminished-Octave Chords and Symbols.* In one chord, the upper of two tones forming an augmented prime functions as the root. In several others, in which certain pairs of tones would form an augmented prime if reduced to adjacency, the resulting upper tone also functions as the root. The lower tone, then, in all of these cases of adjacency, is to be regarded as an inversion of a diminished octave above the root. Chords containing such an interval, or its inversion, are termed "diminished-octave" chords. Three basic types of these chords occur in Op. 19. They, with their abbreviations in parentheses, are termed diminished-octave seventh, ninth, and eleventh chords (7d8, 9d8, and 11d8, respectively). More precisely, the diminished-octave seventh should be described as a seventh chord plus a diminished-octave, but for the sake of a uniform pattern in the terminology, the slightly less accurate expression is retained.

The diminished-octave is represented in chord symbols by a $\flat$8 or a $\natural$8 placed at the right of the chord's Roman numeral. The $\flat$8 is used if the root is diatonic in the prevailing mode (e.g., I$\overset{11}{\underset{\flat 8 \; \flat 5}{\flat 8}}$). The $\natural$8 is used if the root has been raised a semitone above its diatonic counterpart in that mode (e.g., see fig. 3).

5. *Examples of Dual-Membered Tertian and Diminished-Octave Tertian Chords.* Five excerpts are represented. The first of these (example 6; from P.I, mm.6-7) contains two dual-membered fifth chords and an implied dual-membered seventh. The first of the fifth chords (VII$\overset{5}{\underset{\flat 3 \; \flat 3}{\sharp 3}}$) is unusual in that the two forms of its dual member, the third (e$\flat$' and e$\sharp$'), are a doubly augmented prime apart if differences in octave register are ignored. The implied seventh chord (imp VII$\overset{\flat 7}{\underset{\flat 3 \; \flat 3}{\sharp 3}}$) consists of the preceding fifth chord retained in the memory plus a sounding diminished seventh. The other fifth chord is in effect a minor triad plus a diminished fifth, on the raised subdominant (IV$\overset{\sharp 5}{\underset{\natural 1}{\flat 5}}$). These three chords are shown

figure 2

(P.III, m.1: V$\overset{\sharp 5}{\underset{\substack{\sharp 1 \\ \natural 1}}{\substack{\natural 3 \\ \flat 3}}}$)

figure 3

(VII$\overset{\natural 8}{\underset{7 \; \sharp 1}{\substack{7 \\ \sharp 3}}}$)

first in close-position formulations in root position, and then in their compositional configuration (example 6, parts a and b, respectively). In that configuration, the portion of imp VII $^{\flat7}_{\substack{\sharp3\\\flat3}}$ retained in the memory from the preceding chord (VII $^{5}_{\substack{\sharp3\\\flat3\ \flat3}}$) is notated in parenthesized black noteheads.

Example 6

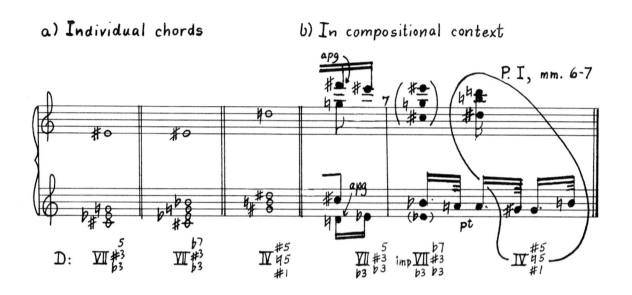

a) **Individual chords**   b) **In compositional context**

A root-position dominant fifth chord having both dual primes and dual thirds (see fig. 4) is shown next (example 7; from P.III, m.1). Ignoring octave register differences, the raised prime (♯1) is a semitone above the root (♮1), and the thirds are minor (♭3) and major (♮3). This chord appears in parenthesized black note-heads because it is a pivot chord in an enharmonically respelled formulation. A root-position tonic seventh chord having minor and major sevenths (♭7 and ♮7, respectively) and a raised fifth (♯5) then follows (I $^{\natural7}_{\substack{\flat7\\\sharp5}}$), succeeded by a submediant fifth chord having minor and major thirds, (♮3 and ♯3, respectively), with the minor third in the bass (VI $^{5}_{\substack{\sharp3\\\natural3\ \natural3}}$). Certain members of the last two chords are presented as parenthesized black noteheads. This is because each is sounding from a previous chord.

figure 4

(V $^{\substack{\sharp5\\\natural3\\\flat3\\\sharp1\\\natural1}}$)

Example 7

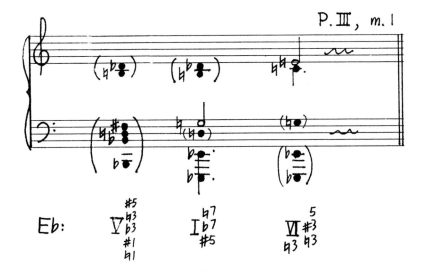

A dual-membered mediant ninth chord in G minor (see fig. 5), having major and minor sevenths (♮7 and ♭7, respectively), the major seventh in the bass, is contained in the third excerpt (example 8; from P.IV, m.12). It is preceded by a tonic minor third chord.

figure 5

$$\left(\mathrm{III}\begin{smallmatrix} \flat 9 \\ \natural 7 \\ \flat 7 \end{smallmatrix} \right)$$
♮7 ♭5

Example 8

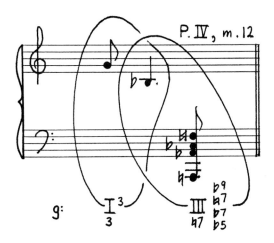

The fourth excerpt (example 9; from **P.I**, mm.16-17) contains a tonic diminished-octave eleventh ($I^{11}_{\flat 8\ \flat 5}$), a tonic dual-membered eleventh ($I^{11}_{\natural 5\ \flat 5}$), and a dominant diminished-octave ninth chord ($V^{\sharp 9}_{\flat 8}$), all within an A♯-Phrygian orientation, a situation which amounts to a rather substantial extension of traditional practice. In the first chord, the diminished-octave member (a♮¹), sounds in an inversion, a semitone below the root (a♯¹). In the second chord, which has a lowered (diminished) and a diatonic (perfect) fifth (♭5 and ♮5, respectively), the diatonic fifth (e♯¹) is in the bass. The third chord is in root position. Example 9 presents these chords individually at first, in white notes and in root position. They are then shown within their compositional context.

Example 9

The final excerpt (example 10; from P.II, mm.6-7) offers a dual-membered thirteenth chord having a lowered (minor) and a raised (augmented) ninth ($\flat$9 and $\sharp$9, respectively), whose third is in the bass and whose root is in the treble ($V^{13}_{\substack{\sharp 9 \\ 3 \, \flat 9}}$). The augmented ninth is regarded as such rather than as a minor third on the basis of the piece's overall harmonic context, which is discussed in chapter IV. In example 10 the chord is shown first in a white-note root-position formulation and then in the compositional configuration of the analysis.

Example 10

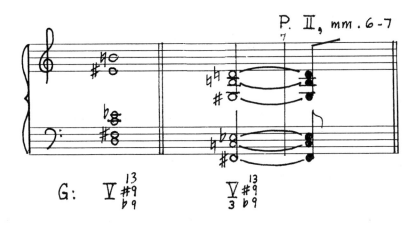

6. *Partially Quartal Chord Symbols.* As is indicated earlier, these chords, when considered from a traditional perspective, can be readily explained as partially quartal arrangements of tertian or dual-membered tertian chords. The symbol used in the identification and description of each such arrangement consists of: (1) the symbol for the tertian or dual-membered tertian chord itself (including an indication of its lowest sounding chord member), as previously described for all tertian and dual-membered tertian chords; (2) a set of diamond-shaped brackets, $\langle \rangle$, enclosing that symbol; and (3) the letters **PQ** preceding the first bracket. For example, $PQ\langle V^{11}_{\substack{\sharp 7 \\ \natural 7}}\rangle$ refers to a partially quartal arrangement of a dual-membered dominant eleventh chord having a diatonic and a raised seventh; $PQ\langle III^{13}_{\substack{\flat 5 \\ \sharp 3}}\rangle$, to a partially quartal arrangement of a tertian mediant thirteenth; and $PQ\langle VII^{13}_{\substack{\sharp 3 \\ 7}}\rangle$, to a partially quartal arrangement of a tertian leading-tone thirteenth whose lowest sounding member is the seventh, indicated by the 7 below the VII.

7. *Examples of Partially Quartal Chords.* Partially quartal chords referred to above are shown in white notation in example 11 (from P.VI, m.1; P.VI, m.5; and P.I, m.7). Each of these is preceded by a root-position close-position formulation, also in white notation, of the tertian or dual-membered tertian chord of which it is a partially quartal arrangement. Broken arrows show how each of these arrangements can be arrived at via transferral of members of the respective tertian or dual-membered tertian chords into different octave-registers.

Example 11

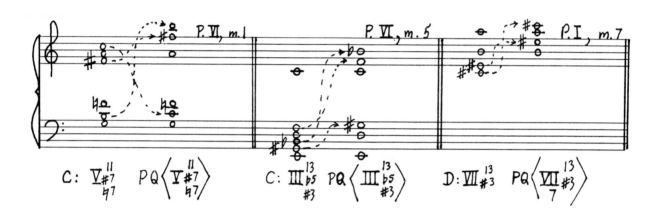

8. *Quartal Chord Symbols.* As with partially quartal chords, symbols used to identify and describe Op. 19's quartal chords reflect a tertian explanation of these chords' derivation, i.e., that the composition's quartal triads are quartal arrangements of tertian elements, and that its quartal tetrads and hexad are quartal arrangements of tertian eleventh chords. The symbol for a quartal triad so regarded is $Q_3\langle TE\rangle$, the letter Q meaning "quartal," the subscript 3 signifying a triad, and the expression $\langle TE\rangle$ referring to the tertian elements which are quartally arranged. The symbol for a quartal tetrad or hexad consists of: (1) the symbol for the tertian eleventh chord itself (including an indication of its lowest sounding chord member); (2) diamond-shaped brackets, $\langle\ \rangle$, enclosing that symbol; and (3) the symbol Q_4 for the tetrad, or Q_6 for the hexad, preceding the first bracket. For example, $Q_4\langle VII^{11}_5\rangle$ refers to a quartal tetrad which is readily explained as a quartal arrangement of a tertian leading-tone eleventh chord whose fifth is its lowest sounding member. Similarly, $Q_6\langle IV^{11}_5\rangle$ signifies a

quartal hexad which is readily explained as a quartal arrangement of a tertian subdominant eleventh whose fifth is also its lowest member.

By analogy with tertian practice, individual members of quartal chords are designated in terms of a "root" and a succession of intervals composed of ascending adjacent fourths above that root, i.e., fourth, seventh, tenth, thirteenth, etc. Just as the root of a tertian chord is the lowest of tertian chord members when these are arranged in ascending adjacent thirds, so the root of a quartal chord is herein regarded as the lowest of quartal chord members when they are arranged in ascending adjacent fourths. As in tertian harmony, if the root of a quartal chord is in the bass, then that chord is in "root position." Alternatively, if the root is not the lowest sounding chord member, and if the chord is still recognizably quartal, then the chord is regarded as being "inverted."

9. *Examples of Quartal Chords.* Three illustrations are offered, one for each of the types of quartal chord referred to above. The first illustration (example 12; from P.I, m.2) shows a quartal triad which consists of tertian elements arranged quartally ($Q_3\langle TE\rangle$). These elements, which constitute the triad's "root" (g♮), "fourth" (c♮'), and "seventh" (f♯'), respectively, are: (1) the seventh (g♮) of a diminished-octave leading-tone seventh chord (see fig 6); (2) a chromatic passing tone with octave displacement (c♮'); and (3) the fifth (f♯') of a tertian tonic fifth chord (I^5). (The octave-displaced chromatic passing tone fills in the motion from the third [c♯'] of the diminished-octave seventh chord to the root of the tonic fifth chord, indicated by a broken arrow.)

figure 6

$$(VII^{\substack{♮8\\7\\7}}_{\substack{♯3\\♯1}})$$

Example 12

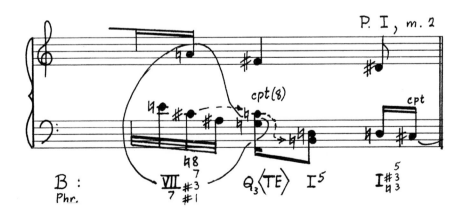

The second illustration (example 13; from P.III, m.3) offers a quartal tetrad ($Q_4\langle VII^{11}_5\rangle$) which can readily be explained as a quartal arrangement of a tertian leading-tone eleventh chord (VII^{11}). In the illustration, this eleventh chord is depicted first of all, in white notation, in root and close position (13a). Then, a close-position quartal arrangement of its members follows, also in white notation (13b). Finally, this arrangement, which is the quartal tetrad itself, is presented in its compositional context, preceded by an eleventh chord on the raised subdominant ($IV^{11}_{\#1}$), succeeded by an implied tonic fifth chord (I^5), and embellished with an appoggiatura (g♯).

Example 13

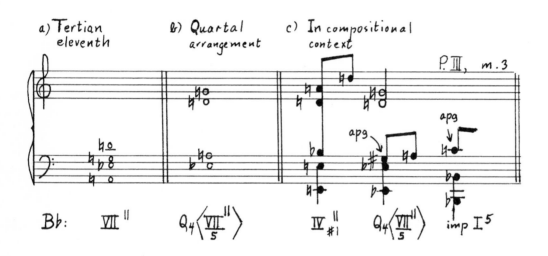

In the third illustration, (example 14; from P.IV, m.11), the composition's sole quartal hexad ($Q_6\langle IV^{11}_5\rangle$) is seen, a chord which can readily be explained as a quartal arrangement of the members of a complete subdominant eleventh chord (IV^{11}). This hexad differs other than structurally from the previously considered triad and tetrad: while they occur in root position in their compositional setting, it does not; its fourth rather than its root is in the bass. In the example, the following are shown, all in white notation: the eleventh chord, in root and close position (14a); a quartal arrangement of its members, in quartal root position (14b); and this arrangement in quartal first inversion as formulated in the composition (14c).

20

Example 14

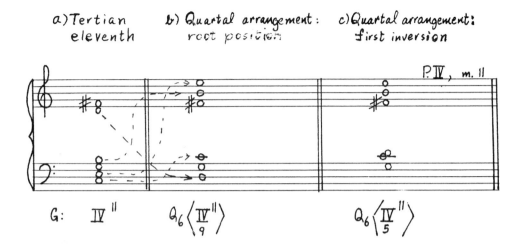

a) Tertian eleventh

b) Quartal arrangement: root position

c) Quartal arrangement: first inversion

P.IV, m. 11

G: IV^{11} Q$_6$⟨$\frac{IV^{11}}{9}$⟩   Q$_6$⟨$\frac{IV^{11}}{5}$⟩

Modulation

Three broad categories of modulation are observed: (1) common chord; (2) common tone; and (3) phrase.

1. *Common Chord.* This type, by far the most prevalent of the three, divides into two sub-types: one which does not involve enharmonic respellings of the pivot chord when changing from orientation about one tonal center to orientation about another; and one which does involve such respelling.

Traditional practice is observed in denoting pivot chords which involve no enharmonic respelling. Two chord-symbols, one above the other, are placed beneath the pivot chord, the top one identifying the chord with reference to the prevailing tonal center (however transient that center's influence may be), and the bottom symbol identifying it with reference to the succeeding center. Thus, in the illustration below (example 15; from P.I, m.8), which pertains to a modulation from D major to G major, the top chord-symbol (II$_{\#3}^{7}$) refers to the pivot chord in terms of the prevailing orientation about D, and the bottom chord-symbol (VI$_{\#3}^{7}$) refers to it in terms of the coming orientation about G.

Example 15

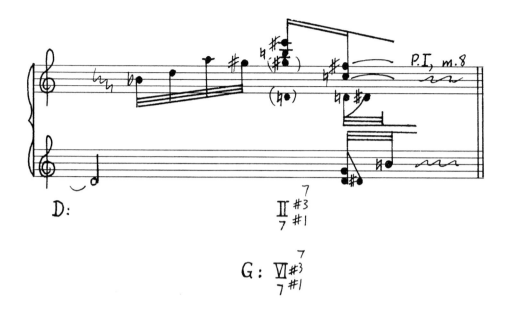

When a common-chord modulation involves enharmonic respelling of the pivot chord, two chord-symbols are still used, as above, but the symbol denoting orientation with reference to the new center is placed below and to the right of the symbol referring to orientation about the prevailing center. Also the pivot chord in its new spelling is shown in parenthesized black noteheads, to the right of the chord in its compositional formulation. This procedure is illustrated in example 16 (from P.III, mm.8-9), in which (1) the pivot chord's symbol in the (temporarily) prevailing orientation of A♭ major (V⁹) is placed below the body of that chord as notated in its A♭ spelling, and (2) the symbol of the respelled pivot chord in its new orientation of G minor (IV♯ii♭¹¹) is placed below and to the right of the A♭ symbol, directly beneath parenthesized black noteheads designating the enharmonic respelling.

In this example, the root (E♭) of the pivot chord as approached (A♭:V⁹) differs from the root (c♯) of that chord as left (g:IV♯ii♭¹¹). This change of root within the chordal structure is an instance of not a root movement but a root shift.

Example 16

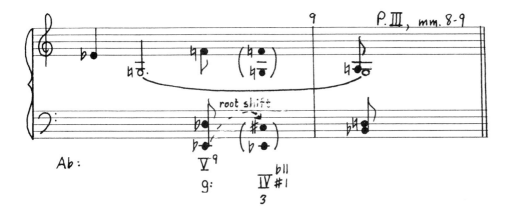

2. *Common Tone*. Two instances of common-tone modulation
occur in Op. 19, one without enharmonic respelling, and one
with it. The first instance (example 17; from P.V, mm.5-7)
involves modulation from a prevailing context of D♭ major to one
of G major. The common tone (a♮[1]) is the major ninth of (1) an
implied diminished-octave chord in D♭ (imp IV$^{\sharp9}_{\natural8}_{\sharp1}$), most of which
appears in parenthesized black noteheads, and (2) a major-minor
ninth chord in G (I$^9_7$).

   Although the aural effect is clearly that of a common-tone
modulation, a case can be made for explaining the implied
diminished-octave ninth chord as a pivot chord which can be
enharmonically respelled with a G orientation. In that case, the
respelled version, represented entirely by parenthesized black
noteheads, and with its symbol also in parentheses, could be
regarded as a dual-membered ninth chord in G major (see fig. 7), or,
with less chromatic alteration in the chord symbol, as such a
chord in G Locrian (sug I$^{\sharp9}_{\natural\sharp7}_{\natural7}$).

   The second instance of common-tone modulation
(example 18; from P.VI, mm.7-8), characterized by enharmonic
respelling of that tone, involves modulation from a D-major
orientation to one of A♭ major. The common tone (d♯ = e♭), an
octave-displaced anticipation, occurs between a horizontalized tonic
third chord in D (I^3) and a solid dominant thirteenth chord in A♭
(see fig. 8). When heard immediately following the third chord,
this tone has the sound of a raised tonic in that orientation
(d♯ =♯1). After the dominant thirteenth chord sounds, the tone is
recognized, retrospectively, as the fifth degree (e♭ = ♮5) of the

figure 7

(sug I$^{9}_{\natural7}_{\flat7}_{\flat5}_{\flat3}$)

figure 8

(V$^{13}_{\natural7}_{\natural7}_{\natural7\sharp5}$)

Example 17

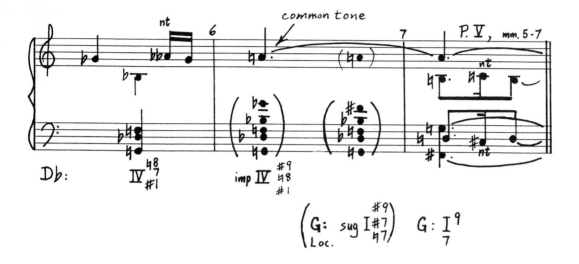

Ab-major scale, and as an octave-displaced anticipation of that
chord's root. Within the body of the chord itself, the root is
preceded by an appoggiatura (fb¹) which may be understood as an
octave-displaced neighbor tone occurring between the octave-
displaced anticipation and the root it anticipates. Incidentally, the
third of this chord (g♮) is also preceded by an appoggiatura (f♯)
which may be understood as an interrupted suspension of the
third of the foregoing third chord in D.

Example 18

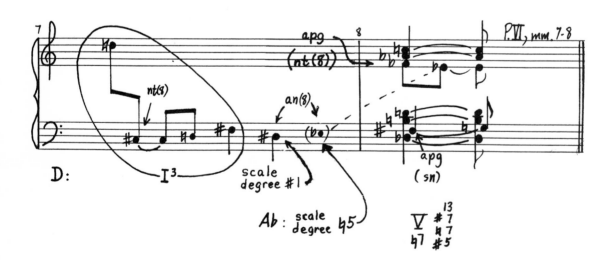

3. *Phrase Modulation.* Two instances of phrase modulation (i.e., modulation characterized by an abrupt change of tonal center at the commencement of a new phrase, without necessary recourse to a pivot chord or common tone from the preceding phrase) are observed (P.III, mm.4-5 and P.IV, mm.9-10). The first of these instances is illustrated in example 19. The "preceding" phrase concludes with a B♭-minor orientation, on a tonic seventh chord (I^7). The "new" phrase, phrase 2 of the piece, commences with a tonic third chord in G major (I^3), and then proceeds via two unaccented appoggiaturas to a partially quartal arrangement of a subdominant thirteenth chord in that orientation. In keeping with the abrupt nature of this type of modulation, the symbol for the new tonal center (G) is simply placed at the beginning of the new phrase, with nothing joining it to symbols of the previous phrase.

Example 19

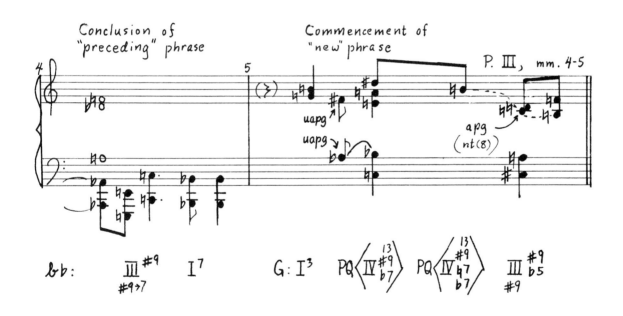

Chord-to-Chord Movement

1. *Simple Succession and Reclassification.* Movement from one chord to another takes place either with or without change of

root.[1] If a root change occurs, it does so in one of two ways: either one root follows another in simple temporal succession, or, in the case of enharmonically respelled pivot chords having one root as approached and another as left, i.e., when root shifts occur, the change of root—as well as that of chord—is essentially one of reclassification rather than of actual temporal succession.

The first three chords of example 20 (D: $\underset{\text{Phr.}}{I}\,{}^{5}_{\sharp 3}\,{}^{5}_{\flat 3}$; C:$VII^{7}_{\flat 1}$; and C:$I^{9}$; from P.I. mm.13-14) illustrate chord-to-chord movement characterized by simple temporal succession of different roots. The third, fourth, and fifth chords (C:I^{9}; C:$I^{9}_{\sharp 5}$; and C:$I^{11}_{\sharp 5}$; from P.I, m.14) show chord-to-chord movement with no change of root. The fifth chord and its enharmonically respelled version appearing in parenthesized black noteheads ($\underset{\text{Phr.}\ \sharp 5}{A\sharp:V^{\sharp 7}_{\sharp 5}}$) illustrate change of chord and of root via reclassification. This version and the passage's final chord ($\underset{\text{Phr.}\ 7}{A\sharp:III^{7}}$) offer a further illustration of chord-to-chord movement characterized by simple succession of different roots.

Example 20

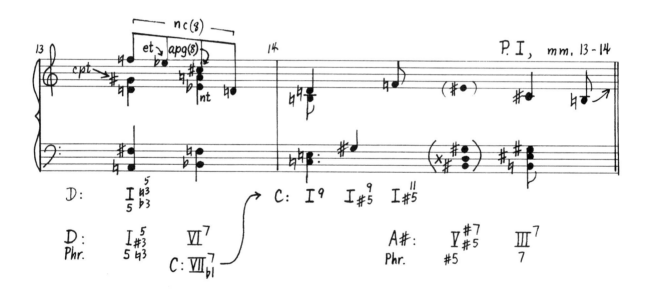

2. *Movement in the Voices.* As chords proceed from one to another, both conjunct and disjunct types of movement are found in the voices involved. Leaps are both large and small. Often a

---

[1] Table 4, in the appendix, provides a list of root movements and shifts taking place within each piece, arranged according to their relative frequency of occurrence.

large leap can be explained as conjunct motion with octave displacement. Lines are often embellished with non-harmonic tones. These features of linear movement are illustrated in example 21 (from P.I., mm.4-5). Small leaps occur there in all voices, as does some conjunct motion; an octave-displaced chromatic passing tone in the treble interjects a wide leap into an otherwise primarily conjunct contour; and a nota cambiata containing both an escape tone and an appoggiatura embellishes the beginning portion of the tenor.

Example 21

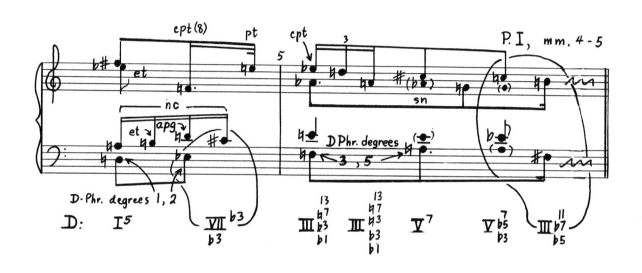

Both conjunct motion and conjunct motion made disjunct through octave displacement are illustrated in a progression shown in example 22 (from P.I., mm.7-8). Two chords are involved: (1) a partially quartal arrangement of a tertian leading-tone thirteenth ($PQ\langle VII_{7}^{13}_{\#3}\rangle$); and (2) a quartal arrangement of a tertian tonic eleventh ($Q_{4}\langle I^{11}\rangle$). These chords are shown: (1) as tertian harmonies in root and close position, in solid form, arranged neither quartally nor partially so (22a); (2) in their partially quartal and quartal arrangements, respectively, but in solid form (22b); and (3) in their rhythmic formulation as in the composition (22c). Basic conjunct motion in all voices, with no octave displacement, is seen in 22a. Then in 22b, while two of the voices still move conjunctly, the other two undergo octave displacement. Finally, in 22c, the conjunct motion of the two voices and the disjunct motion of the other two are expressed in their compositional context.

Example 22

Another chord-to-chord movement, the composition's first progression, offers a further illustration of conjunct motion made disjunct through octave displacement, except here the conjunct motion is more subtly concealed. The progression consists of two chords: (1) a leading-tone ninth of B Phrygian (VII^9); and (2) a submediant fifth chord of B major (VI^5). Example 23 (from P.I, m.1 and its pickup) shows the progression: (1) in its basic form (23a); (2) with octave displacement in the lower two voices (23b); and (3) in its compositional formulation (23c).

Example 23

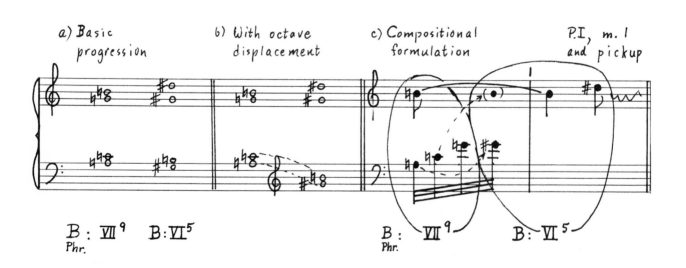

3. *Overlapping.* From time to time, chords overlap, a condition illustrated in example 24 (from P.I, m.1). There, in a continuation of the passage cited in example 23, parts of the tonic fifth chord of B major (I^{5}_{3}) and of the supertonic fifth chord of B Phrygian (II^{5}_{3}) sound together as indicated by the curved enclosures surrounding the notes of those chords.

The composition's first quartal chord, a triad ($\mathrm{Q}_{3}\langle\mathrm{TE}\rangle$), comes about in conjunction with these chords' overlapping. Specifically, this chord originates through the concurrence of the following tertian elements: (1) the fifth of the Phrygian supertonic fifth chord (g♮); (2) that chord's root (c♮'); and (3) the appoggiatura (e♯')—which is also an altered passing tone with octave displacement in the motion from the tonic chord's third (d♯'') to its fifth (f♯')—enharmonically respelled as f♮', as in the score.

Example 24

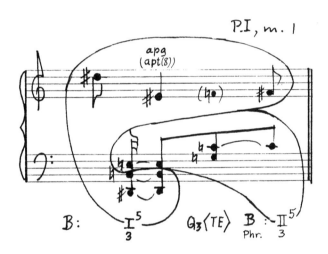

As is indicated above, the present study's primary exposition of Op. 19's harmonic organization is a set of six harmonic analyses—one for each piece. The foregoing consideration of chord-to-chord movement completes this chapter's intended introduction to the symbolization employed in these analyses and to the musical organization which they reveal. Accordingly, it is now appropriate to proceed to the analyses themselves, in the next chapter, "Six Harmonic Analyses."

Study of the piece's harmonic organization should take place with ready access to a piano and with the score at hand. The analyses have been developed through prolonged and intense aural as well as visual and conceptual involvement with this composition, and what they have to offer can be most fruitfully absorbed through involvement with them in the same three-fold fashion.

III Six Harmonic Analyses

The preceding chapter, while offering an introduction to the analyses, does not deal with the harmonic organization of entire individual pieces. That is reserved for the present chapter, wherein (1) the pieces are briefly described verbally in turn, with reference to features of the organization manifested by each, and (2) the organization of each piece is explained in detail, via the analyses themselves.

Verbal Summary

Piece I is the largest and harmonically most complex of the six. It consists of four phrases of unequal duration; is organized with reference to seven tonal centers; manifests primarily two modal orientations, viz., major and Phrygian; and of all the composition's pieces, exhibits the richest harmonic vocabulary. The modal orientation about the piece's initial tonal center is largely Phrygian; that about its final center is solely so.

Piece II, the only one of the six in which modulation does not occur, is harmonically one of the work's two least complex and most static pieces, the other being piece VI. It consists of two phrases and is conspicuous for a much reiterated tonic third chord.

Piece III, comprising two phrases linked by a phrase modulation, is organized about six tonal centers, four of them being in the first phrase. Dual-membered chords occur prominently. Quartal and partially quartal chords are also present. Most of the chords are found in solid form.

Piece IV, perhaps the most volatile of the pieces rhythmically and harmonically, consists of three phrases; is also organized with reference to six tonal centers; and has a texture in which (1) a single melodic strand outlines various relatively simple harmonies, occasionally only suggesting them, and (2) generally complex solid chords offer emphatic contrast.

Piece V, which comprises three phrases, is one of the composition's tonally more stable pieces. Until near the end of the third phrase, it is organized with reference to only two centers. There a change to a third center occurs, followed quickly by another change to a fourth. The harmonic vocabulary is very complex, although containing no quartal or partially quartal chords; however it is less rich than that of piece I.

Piece VI, consisting of two phrases organized about three tonal centers, or about four of them if the final tonal orientation of piece V is heard to be retained at the beginning of piece VI, is conspicuous for its lingeringly slow harmonic rhythm and for bell-like sounds resulting from third-less seventh chords and abundant partially quartal elevenths.

Analysis I - Piece I

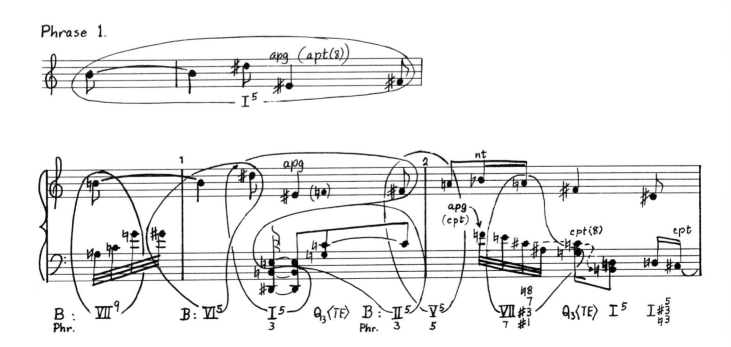

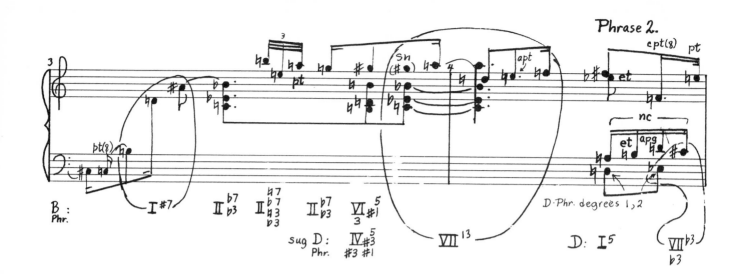

Phrase 2.

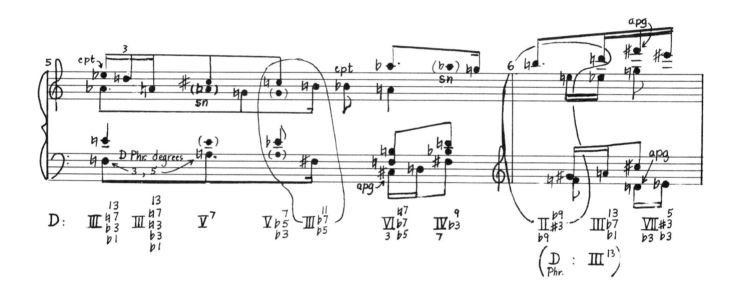

Phrase 3.

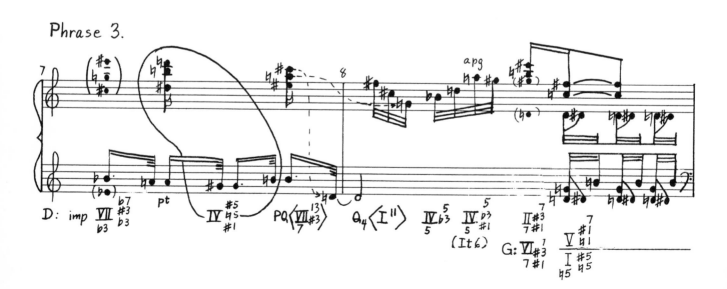

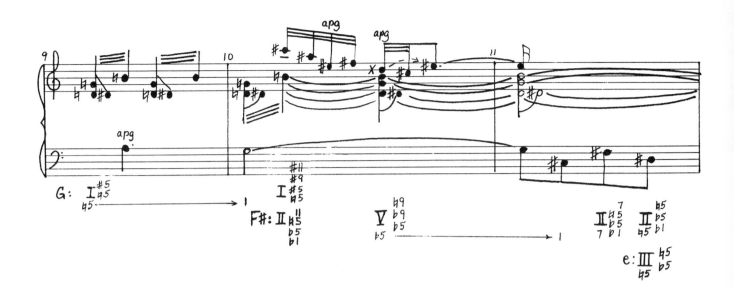

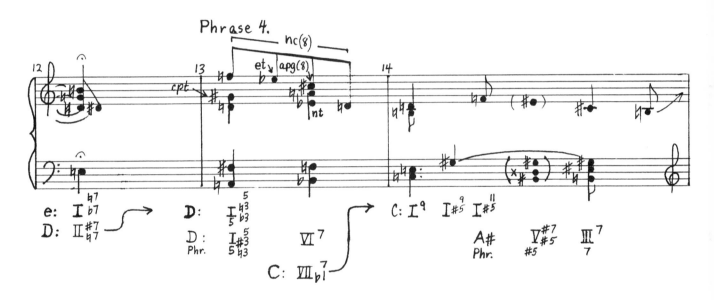

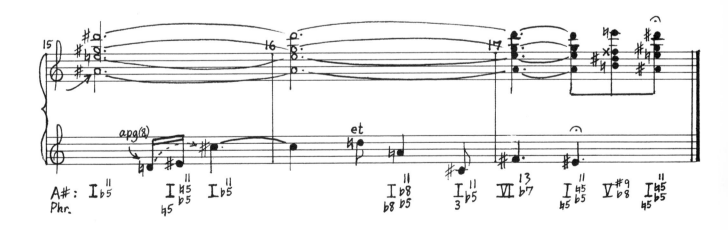

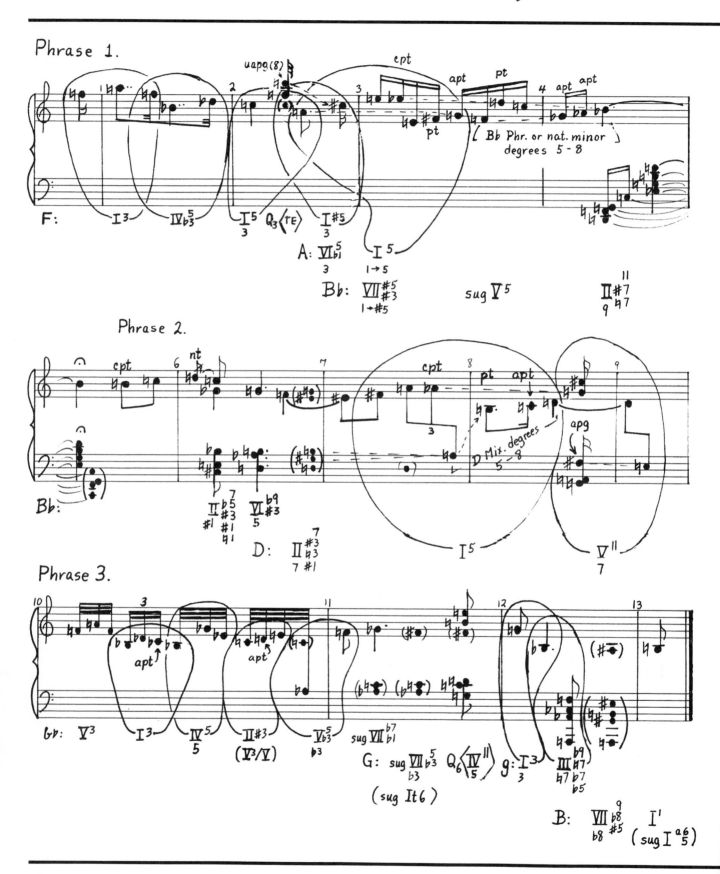

IV Underlying Relationships

The Op. 19 pieces, although brief, manifest complex relationships which extend well below the surface of the music. Four striking instances of such relationships are explored in the present chapter. The first of these involves a quasi-Schenkerian explanation of piece II in terms of unfoldment, in stages, of a fundamental "background" progression or Ursatz; the second deals with derivation of piece VI from an underlying tertian formulation; the third pertains to patterns observed in the succession of the composition's tonal centers; and the fourth, to patterns in the succession of harmonic roots.

Piece II: Ursatz and Unfoldment

Under structure-prolongation analysis, piece II reduces to a four-chord progression which derives from a three-chord Ursatz. The Ursatz, the progression, and a stage in the latter's derivation from the former are shown in example 25. In this example and the next, principal chords are represented in whole notes, and items of embellishment are given as black noteheads. Voice-leading movement is indicated by broken arrows.

Example 25

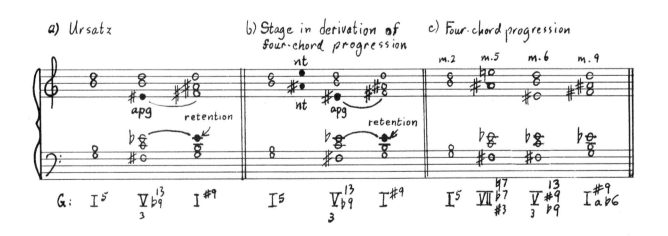

The unfoldment which occurs in the course of proceeding from the four-chord progression to the piece itself involves: (1)

passing, neighboring, and other embellishing motions; (2)
rearrangement of notes in regard to octave register; and (3)
overlapping. Three intermediate stages in this unfoldment are
represented in example 26. In the first of these (26a), preliminary
prolongation occurs, largely via passing and neighboring motion,
and with some octave displacement. In the second (26b),
overlapping, further embellishment, and additional
rearrangement as to octave register take place. In the third (26c),
all remaining octave displacements are effected.

Example 26

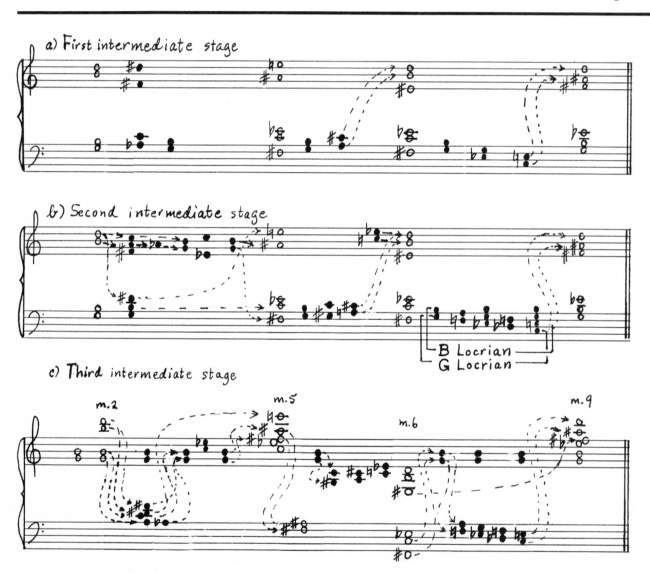

Transition from the stage represented by example 26c to the
piece itself takes place by clothing the pitches of that stage with
rhythm and by adding any needed melodic details (example 27).

Example 27

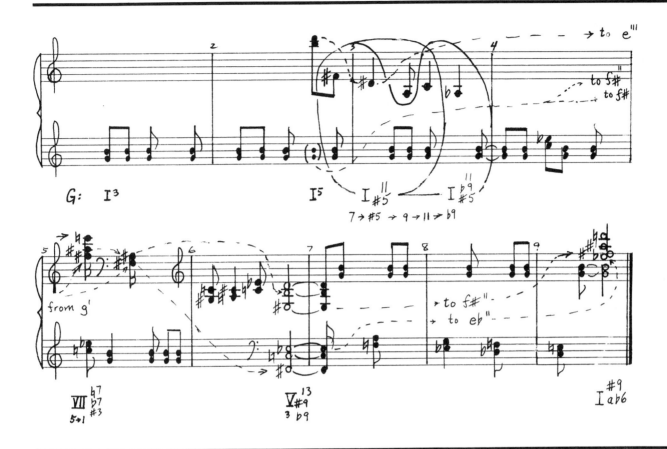

Derivation of Piece VI from an Underlying Tertian Formulation

The tertian formulation from which piece VI can be derived
is based primarily on two progressions, the first of which occurs
singly, and the second, in combination with the first (example 28).

Example 28

The underlying formulation itself is presented in example 29. Broken bar lines there do not necessarily coincide with bar lines in the score, but rather set off harmonic units and progressions. The distance from one broken bar line to the next may be termed a "pseudo measure." As the piece itself consists of two phrases, so does this formulation. The tonal context of the first phrase is that of C major; the tonal context of the second is that of D major followed by that of A♭ major. The first phrase contains three statements of basic progression 1, the third of which (pseudo measure 3) occurs in combination with basic progression 2 as in example 28d. The second phrase also contains a statement of both basic progressions combined (pseudo measure 7), but within an A♭ major context, and proceeding to tonic harmony in that key.

Example 29

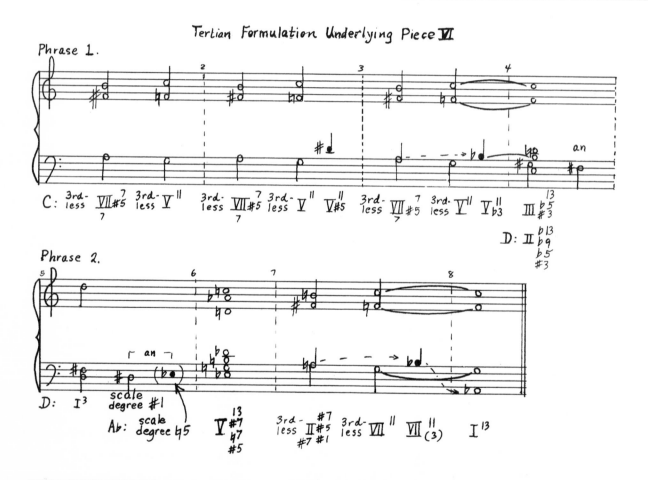

Between the underlying formulation and the piece itself is a modification of the former effected by means of octave displacement, quartal rearrangement, and overlapping. These processes are illustrated in the next three examples, in which the derivation of two partially quartal hexads and a quartal tetrad is shown.

The first hexad, a partially quartal arrangement of a dominant eleventh chord with minor and major sevenths $(\text{PQ}\left\langle V^{11}_{\sharp 7 \natural 7}\right\rangle)$, derives from basic progression 1 (example 30). Through octave displacement in all voices of the progression, the second chord is rearranged as a quartal triad (30b). Then, via overlapping of the progression's first chord with the quartal rearrangement of its second, the partially quartal arrangement of the dual-membered eleventh chord comes into being (30c). The eleventh chord itself, termed "ancestral," is shown in root and close position in example 30d.

Example 30

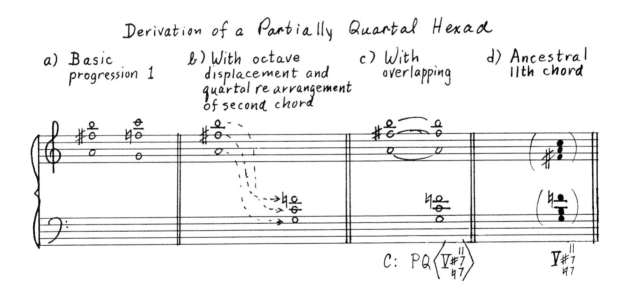

Derivation of a Partially Quartal Hexad

a) Basic progression 1   b) With octave displacement and quartal rearrangement of second chord   c) With overlapping   d) Ancestral 11th chord

The quartal tetrad $(\text{Q}_4\left\langle V^{11}_{\flat 3}\right\rangle)$ may be regarded as a quartal arrangement of the combined second chords of the two basic progressions, it being understood that the chords so combined constitute the tetrad's ancestral eleventh chord. This arrangement comes about in two stages, which are illustrated in example 31. First, via octave displacement in all voices of progression 1, the second chord of that progression is rearranged as a quartal triad (31b). This triad and the sustained first chord of progression 2 overlap to form another instance of the partially quartal hexad

43

described above ($PQ\langle V^{11}_{\sharp 7}\rangle$). While the quartal triad is sustained, the second chord of progression 2 is rearranged as a second quartal triad, via octave displacement in two of the progression's voices. The two quartal triads overlap, a result of which is formation of the quartal tetrad (31b). The ancestral eleventh chord of which the tetrad is a quartal arrangement is shown in example 31c.

Example 31

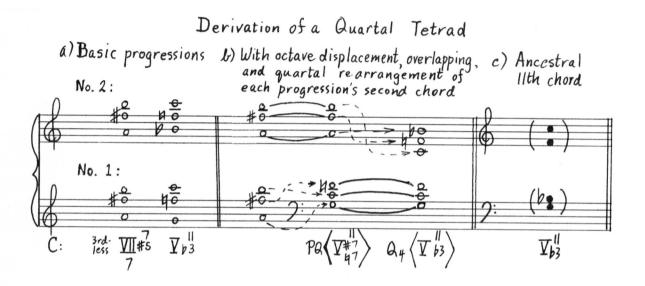

Derivation of a Quartal Tetrad

a) Basic progressions   b) With octave displacement, overlapping,   c) Ancestral 11th chord
and quartal re-arrangement of each progression's second chord

The second partially quartal hexad ($PQ\langle III^{13}_{\flat 5}\rangle$) derives via oblique motion from the two quartal triads which constitute the foregoing quartal tetrad. While the top triad is sustained, the members of the bottom one move, one conjunctly, and the other two by motion which would be conjunct if it were not for octave displacement. Example 32a shows the oblique motion without octave displacement, and example 32b shows this motion with it. The thirteenth chord, of which the hexad is a partially quartal arrangement, is represented in root and close position in example 32c.

Example 32

Derivation of a Partially Quartal Hexad

a) $Q_4 \left\langle \underset{b3}{\overset{11}{V}} \right\rangle$ and its
oblique continuation

b) Continuation with
octave displacement

c) 13th chord
in root and
close position

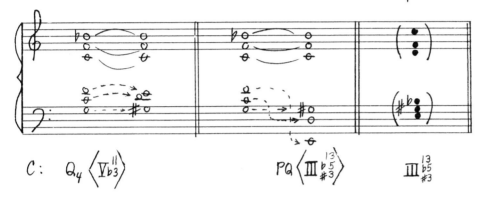

$C: \quad Q_4 \left\langle \underset{b3}{\overset{11}{V}} \right\rangle$

$PQ \left\langle \underset{\#3}{\overset{13}{III}} \underset{b5}{} \right\rangle$

$\underset{\#3}{\overset{13}{III}} \underset{b5}{}$

Having illustrated the processes of octave displacement, quartal rearrangement, and overlapping, it is appropriate to present the entire underlying formulation as modified by these processes, in order that (1) the formulation and its modification can be compared and (2) the role of these processes in modifying any part of the formulation can be readily perceived (example 33). To facilitate such comparison, broken bar lines bounding pseudo measures, in exact correspondence with broken bar lines of example 29, are included. Transition from the modification to the piece itself as shown in analysis VI comes about primarily by imbuing the pitches of the modification with rhythm, and by adding such melodic details as may be needed.

Example 33

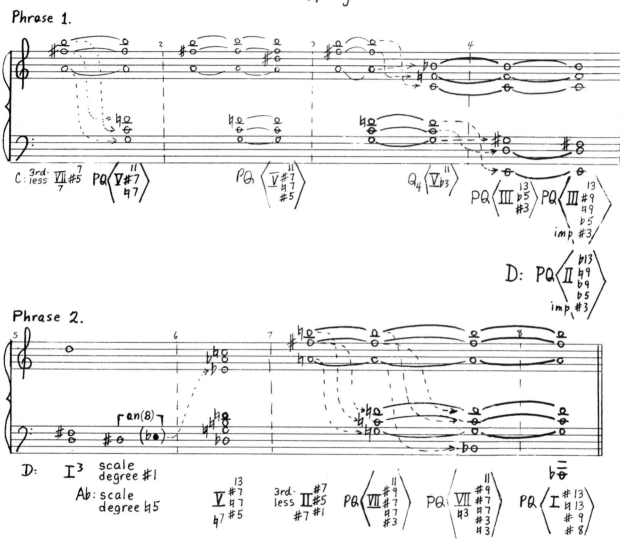

Modification of
Tertian Formulation Underlying Piece VI,
Via Octave Displacement, Quartal Rearrangement,
and Overlapping

Patterns in the Succession of Tonal Centers

One of the study's most unexpected discoveries is that within
the succession of tonal centers of each piece—excepting II, which
has only one center—and of the composition as a whole, patterns
exist which clearly refer to a traditional mode or scale, which

outline or suggest traditional tertian chords, and which imply traditional harmonic movement. A consideration of these patterns follows, first with reference to individual pieces, and then with reference to the composition in its entirety.

1. *Piece I.* In this piece, seven centers (B D G F♯ E D C A♯) outline an ascending G-major triad in first inversion, an ensuing scalewise descent through a perfect fifth, and a further descent of a diminished third (example 34). When repeated without pause, this pattern is clearly heard to have a B-Phrygian orientation. Harmonies implied are the G-major triad mentioned (VI^{5}_{3}) and a German sixth chord on A♯ ($\text{VII}^{7}_{♯1}$).

Example 34

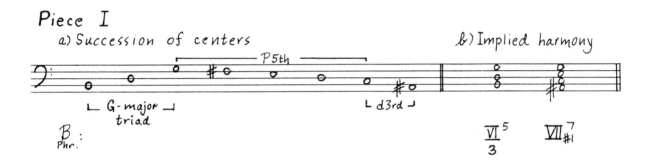

2. *Piece III.* Here seven centers (B E♭ F B♭ G A♭ G) suggest a two-voice texture within an E♭-major context (example 35). The lower voice descends through a semitone to the dominant, and the upper voice rises from the tonic to the subdominant and then returns to the mediant. Harmony implied is that of a half-diminished seventh chord on the supertonic ($\text{II}^{7}_{♭5♭5}$) and a tonic triad in second inversion (I^{5}_{5}). The A♭ in the upper voice functions as a neighbor tone.

Example 35

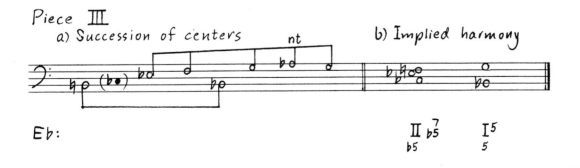

3. *Piece IV*. Piece IV's tonal centers, six in number (F A B♭ D B♭ G B) also suggest a two-voice texture (example 36). If the pattern is heard in isolation, its tonal context is ambiguous, F, B♭, and E♭ major being possible orientations. However, when this pattern follows the pattern of piece III, the orientation is heard to be that of E♭ major. The upper voice consists of three scale degrees: the second, seventh, and third, in that order. The lower also comprises three members, rising chromatically: a raised subdominant, a dominant which is repeated, and a raised dominant. Chords implied are: a dyad functioning as a dominant of the dominant (V^3/V); a dominant triad (V^5); a mediant triad (III^5_3); and a mediant triad with a raised third ($III^5_{\#3}$).

Example 36

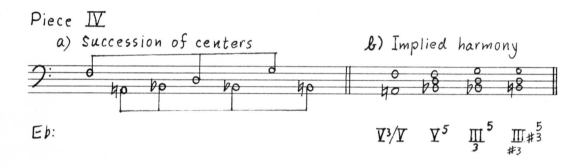

Piece IV
  a) Succession of centers   b) Implied harmony

E♭: V^3/V V^5 III^5_3 $III^5_{\#3}$

4. *Piece V*. Here are four centers (D♭ G B♭ E) which constitute a diminished seventh chord (example 37). Heard in isolation, the chord is tonally ambiguous: heard within the E♭-major context of the two preceding patterns, it can be understood as occurring on the raised tonic ($I^7_{\#1}$).

Example 37

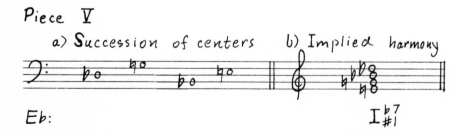

Piece V
  a) Succession of centers   b) Implied harmony

E♭: $I^{♭7}_{\#1}$

5. *Piece VI.* Piece VI has only three centers—four if the final orientation from piece V is retained (example 38). These three (C D A♭), when heard by themselves, have no particular melodic shape, but they do suggest a half-diminished seventh chord having D as its root. Within an E♭-major context, this would be a leading-tone chord (VII[7]).

Example 38

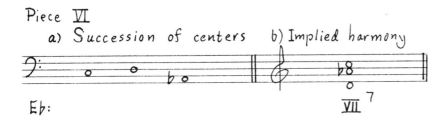

Piece VI
a) Succession of centers   b) Implied harmony

E♭:   VII[7]

6. *Overall Pattern of Centers from Pieces I-VI.* Op. 19's tonal centers, taken in their natural order of succession, can readily be formed into a single overall pattern which integrates the patterns from pieces I, III, and IV and the single center from piece II in a musically meaningful fashion and provides an appropriate melodic shape for the succession of centers of pieces V and VI. Texturally this pattern manifests a ternary organization comprising monophonic first and third parts and a second part in which two voices are suggested. The first part has a B-Phrygian orientation; the second and third parts have an E♭-major one. The pattern does not end with any sense of finality, harmonically or rhythmically. Rather, it is open-ended and leads readily back to its beginning. It can thus be repeated endlessly. The pattern is represented in example 39. There, individual patterns from the five pieces and the single center from piece II are set off by broken bar lines and labelled according to their source pieces with abbreviations P.I through P.VI.

Example 39

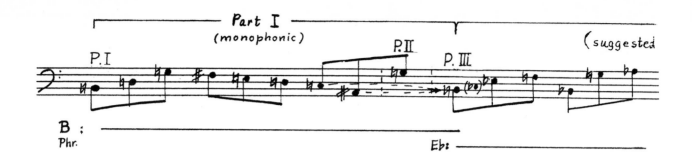

7. *Linear Contours in the Overall Pattern.* Implicit in the succession of tonal centers, and in the melodic pattern when its vertical range is reduced to an octave bounded by Ab's, are three linear contours, one of which is conjunct in nature while the other two are primarily so. These contours, which contain all of the succession's tonal centers, are shown in example 40, each being represented by half notes joined by an extended beam. As in example 39, the particular piece to which each center or group of centers belongs is indicated by broken bar lines and the abbreviations P.I through P.VI.

Example 40

Conjunct and Primarily Conjunct
Contours in Succession of Tonal Centers

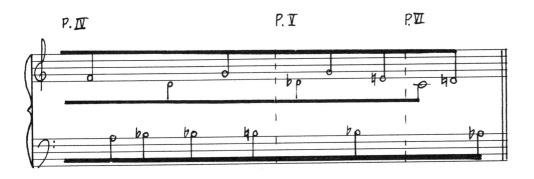

8. *Three-Voice Passage Realized from the Linear Contours.*
Sometimes successive centers of a contour follow each other
immediately (e.g., piece I, contour 3: notes g¹, f#¹, and e¹). On the
other hand, a particular center in a given contour must often
await the occurrence of movement in one or both of the other
contours before it can move to its own successor in its own
contour (e.g., in piece I the first center of contour 1 [b] does not
proceed to that contour's second center [a#] until after movement
involving the above-mentioned three centers of contour 3 has
occurred and the first center of contour 2 [d¹] has been repeated
and has moved to c¹).

However, if within each contour, every center which must
await the occurrence of movement in another contour before
proceeding to its successor in its own is sustained physically for

the duration of that wait (e.g., if the b which commences contour 1 is sustained until the succeeding a♯ occurs, if the d¹ which commences contour 2 is sustained until that center is repeated, etc.), then a three-voice passage whose harmonic vocabulary and movement comply by and large with nineteenth-century chromatic practice results. This passage is shown in example 41, accompanied by an abbreviated harmonic analysis and an indication, via broken-line enclosures and abbreviations P.I through P.VI, of the piece to which each center belongs.

Example 41

As is the case with the melodic pattern of example 39, this passage is organized about two tonal centers, and ends abruptly with no sense of harmonic finality. However, its centers are G and Eb rather than B and Eb, a difference which can be explained in that while the B-Phrygian orientation in the pattern results largely from melodic emphasis upon B, in a context which otherwise would be that of G major, the harmony of the corresponding portion of the passage does not emphasize that center, and the G-major context is heard to prevail.

9. *Susceptibility of the Three-Voice Passage to Repetition.* Like its monophonic parent-pattern (example 39), the three-voice passage is also self-repeating. However, here two modes of repetition are possible. The first, characterized by maximum linear economy in proceeding from the passage to its first repetition and from one repetition to the next, is such that if contours 1, 2, and 3 are represented by symbols C_1, C_2, and C_3, respectively, and if downward displacement of contours by successive octaves is indicated by subscripts 8, 15, 22, etc., then contours proceed from one to another according to the following pattern:

$$C_3 \rightarrow C_2 \rightarrow C_1 \rightarrow C_{3_8} \rightarrow C_{2_8} \rightarrow C_{1_8} \rightarrow C_{3_{15}} \rightarrow C_{2_{15}} \rightarrow C_{1_{15}} \rightarrow C_{3_{22}} \rightarrow C_{2_{22}} \rightarrow C_{1_{22}}, \text{ etc.}$$

Transition from the conclusion of the passage to the commencement of its first repetition is illustrated in example 42, with C_3 proceeding to C_2 in the top voice, C_2 to C_1 in the middle voice, and C_1 to C_{3_8} in the bottom one.

Example 42

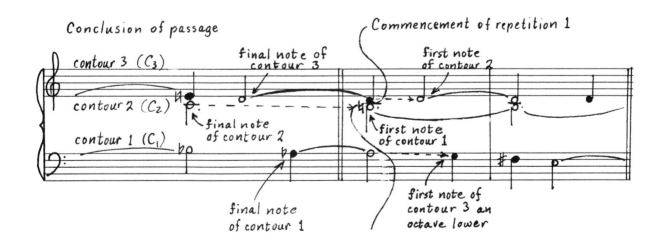

Conclusion of passage

Commencement of repetition 1

contour 3 (C_3)

final note of contour 3

first note of contour 2

contour 2 (C_2)

final note of contour 2

first note of contour 1

contour 1 (C_1)

final note of contour 1

first note of contour 3 an octave lower

a) *Rotation of Contours: Progressive Overall Descent.* Two important features of repetition according to this mode are (1) "rotation" of the contours through the three voices, i.e., ascent of the contours from the bottom and middle voices into the middle and top voices, respectively, and descent of the contour from the top voice into the bottom voice, and (2) progressive lowering of overall pitch with each successive repetition. These features are illustrated in example 43, where the location of contours in the original passage and its first three repetitions is shown. With the third repetition a complete rotation is seen to have taken place: the contours have returned to their original voices and pitch in each voice, and thus in the repetition as a whole, is an octave lower than originally.

Example 43

	Original passage	Repetition 1	Repetition 2	Repetition 3
top voice	$C_3 \longrightarrow$	$C_2 \longrightarrow$	$C_1 \longrightarrow$	C_{3_8}
middle voice	$C_2 \longrightarrow$	$C_1 \longrightarrow$	$C_{3_8} \longrightarrow$	C_{2_8}
bottom voice	$C_1 \longrightarrow$	$C_{3_8} \longrightarrow$	$C_{2_8} \longrightarrow$	C_{1_8}

Theoretically the contour-succession pattern can go on endlessly, as can therefore repetitions of the passage. However, because of the descent associated with each such repetition, the threshold of pitch audibility is soon reached, thereby placing a limit upon the number of repetitions which can have any practical significance.

b) *Rotation of Voices: No Overall Descent.* The above-mentioned difficulty can be avoided by introducing upward octave-displacement into the movement from contour 1 to its successor. That successor will then be contour 3, untransposed, and the contour-succession pattern will read as follows, upward octave-displacement being indicated by 8's placed above arrows:

$$C_3 \rightarrow C_2 \rightarrow C_1 \overset{8}{\rightarrow} C_3 \rightarrow C_2 \rightarrow C_1 \overset{8}{\rightarrow} C_3, \text{ etc.}$$

This pattern underlies the second mode of repetition. Accordingly, in that mode, the transition from the conclusion of the passage to the commencement of the first repetition is identical, contour-wise, with the transition from the conclusion of any repetition to the commencement of the next repetition.

These transitions are represented in example 44, with specific reference to the conclusion of the passage and the commencement of the first repetition. There, the final note of contour 1 (a♭) does not fall to the first note (g) of a downward transposed contour 3, but rather proceeds, by a falling second and a simultaneous upward octave-displacement, to the first note (g¹) of an untransposed contour 3.

Example 44

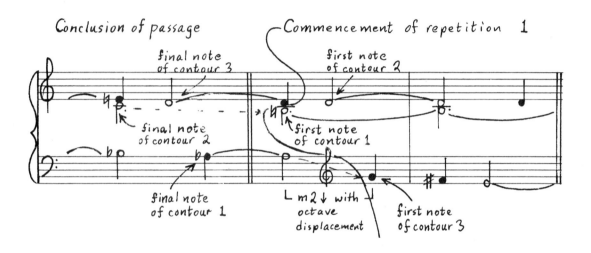

Introduction of upward octave-displacement into the movement from contour 1 to contour 3 has a three-fold effect. First, it results in a contour-succession pattern which can continue without limit. Second, it provides a way in which the passage can be repeated endlessly, free of encumbrance from a pitch audibility threshold. Third, it changes rotation of contours through the voices (example 43) into rotation of voices through the contours.

Rotation of voices through the contours, i.e., systematic movement of each voice from one contour to the next, is illustrated in example 45. There the contours are to be understood as being fixed in position, one above another, and the three voices, represented by symbols V_1, V_2, and V_3, pass from contour to contour as indicated by arrows.

Example 45

	Passage	Repetition 1	Repetition 2	Repetition 3
contour 3:	V_3	V_1	V_2	V_3
contour 2:	V_2	V_3	V_1	V_2
contour 1:	V_1	V_2	V_3	V_1

} etc.

Patterns in the Succession of Harmonic Roots

The inherent susceptibility of the succession of tonal centers to ready polyphonic arrangement finds a striking counterpart in a similar quality discovered in the succession of harmonic roots. Thus, in each of the six pieces, the roots, taken in their natural order of occurrence, form patterns which suggest largely three-voice tonal passages. These passages consist essentially of non-disjunct contours in combination, and comply by and large with nineteenth-century harmonic practice.

The pieces' six root-successions and a polyphonic passage derived from each succession appear in examples 46-51. Therein, root-to-root movement in each succession is indicated by more or less standard interval-abbreviations coupled generally with arrows showing ascent and descent (e.g., P4↑ indicates an ascending perfect fourth, m3↓ a descending minor third, tt a tritone, etc.). To facilitate comparison of each succession and the corresponding polyphonic passage, all roots are numbered. Additionally, a minimal harmonic analysis accompanies each such passage. In keeping with the tonal context of the passage, notes therein will often be respelled as enharmonic equivalents of their counterparts in the succession.

1. *Piece I.* The roots of piece I suggest a three-voice tonal passage characterized by: (1) imitation in the voices' initial entries; (2) chordal and linear chromaticism; (3)modulation from the mediant (D♭) to the dominant (F) to the tonic of B♭ minor (these centers forming a minor triad); and (4) ready repeatability (example 46).

Example 46

Piece I   a) Succession of roots

Phrase 1

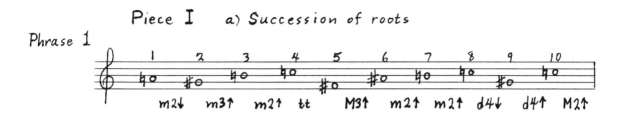

Phrase 2

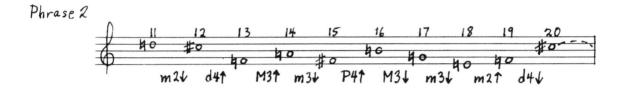

Phrase 3

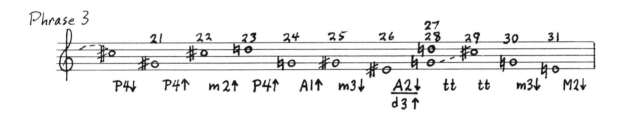

Phrase 4

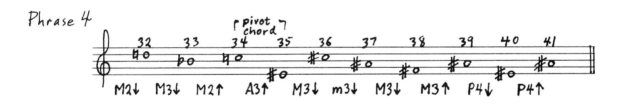

Piece I   b) Suggested polyphonic passage

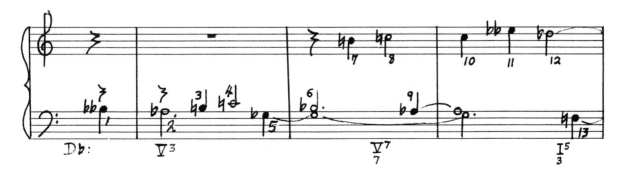

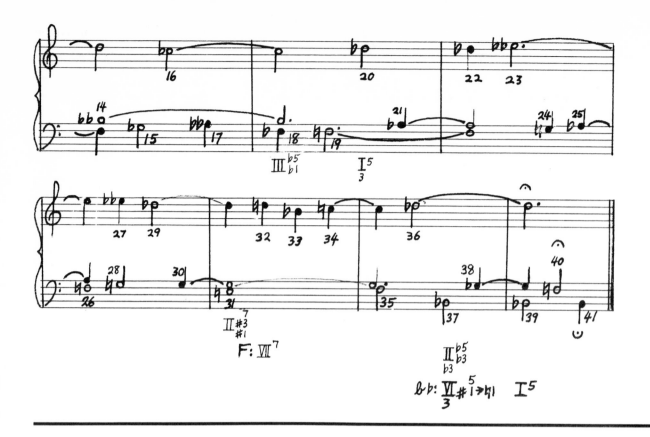

2. *Piece II*. The roots of piece II outline a slightly embellished C-minor triad, primarily in two voices (example 47).

Example 47

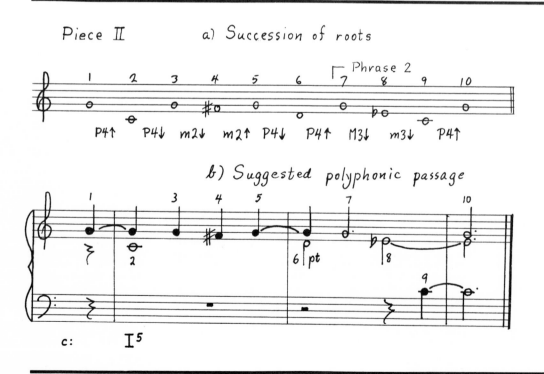

3. *Piece III*. From the root succession of piece III, a highly chromatic three-voice passage is derived which modulates through a tritone (E♭ major to A major), a descending perfect fourth (A major to E minor), and an ascending diminished fourth (E major to A♭ minor). This passage is readily repeatable. With some enharmonic respelling, the four centers represented, taken in order of occurrence, suggest the tritone D♯-A and its resolution E-G♯. The succession of roots, the polyphonic passage, and the tritone and its resolution are shown in example 48, parts a, b, and c, respectively.

Example 48

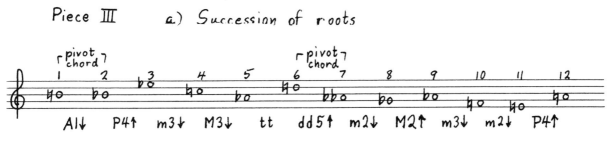

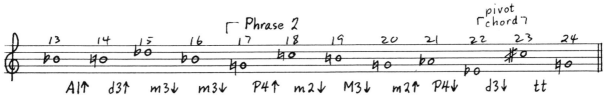

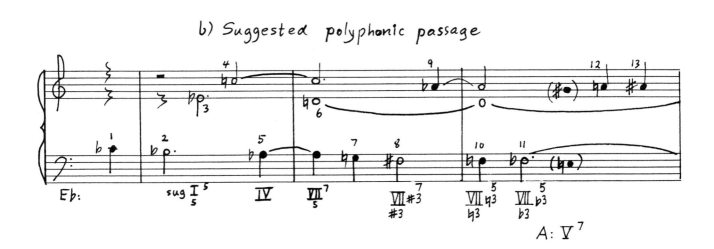

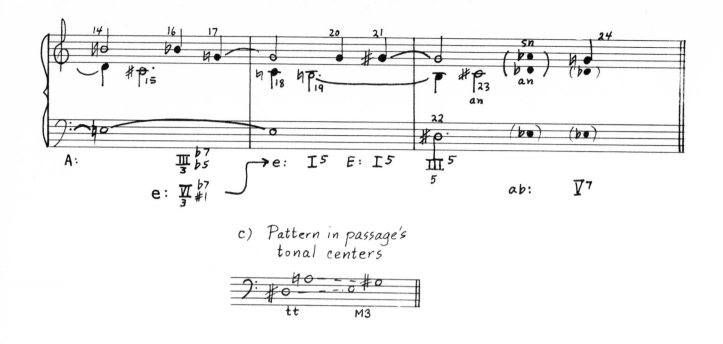

c) Pattern in passage's
tonal centers

4. *Piece IV.* From the root succession of piece IV, a slightly chromatic passage having primarily three voices is obtained (example 49). In this passage, F serves as a tonal center and E♭ as a suggested one. If the passage is heard immediately after the passage derived from the roots of piece III is heard, then the A♭ minor orientation from the conclusion of that passage is briefly retained (indicated in parentheses).

Example 49

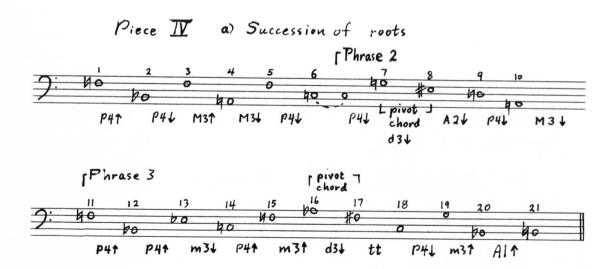

b) Suggested polyphonic passage

(ab: sug II#5, if
orientation from end of
previous passage is
retained)

F: I⁵₃

IV⁵

sug Eb: I⁵₅

---

5. *Piece V.* The passage suggested by piece V's succession of roots
consists of three voices, commences in B♭ minor, quickly proceeds
to E♭ major and remains therein, exhibits considerable
chromaticism in its inner voice, includes a quartal triad in its
harmonic vocabulary, and is readily repeatable (example 50).

Example 50

Piece V   a) Succession of roots

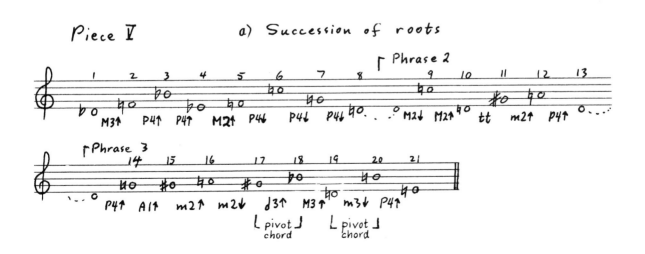

61

b) Suggested polyphonic passage

$bb: \text{I}^5_3$

sug $Eb: \text{VI}^5_3 \quad Q_3\langle TE\rangle \quad Eb:\text{VII}^7$

$\text{V}^7_3 \qquad \text{VII}^{b7}_{b3}$

$(Gn6)$

---

6. *Piece VI.* The roots of piece VI suggest a passage whose tonal center is G until the final chord, when it becomes Ab (example 51). Approximately half of the passage consists of two voices; the remainder consists of three.

Example 51

Piece VI   a) Succession of roots

M3↓   M3↑   M3↓   M3↑   M3↓   m3↓   M2↓   m2↑   d4↓   M3↓   m2↑

b) Suggested polyphonic passage

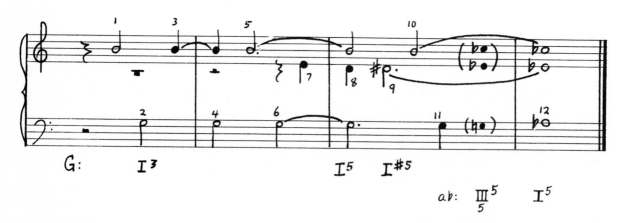

$G: \qquad \text{I}^3 \qquad\qquad\qquad\qquad \text{I}^5 \quad \text{I}^{\#5}$

$ab: \text{III}^5_5 \quad \text{I}^5$

The six polyphonic passages deriving from root successions proceed readily from one to another in consecutive order, and from the sixth passage to the first. These passages may thus be regarded as members of a theoretically endlessly repeatable cycle.

Consideration of these passages marks the conclusion of the detailed exposition of Op. 19's harmonic organization which began in chapter II. Now, having introduced and presented the six harmonic analyses and explored underlying relationships, it is desirable to bring the findings of the study into perspective. This is done in the fifth and final chapter, "Perspectives."

V Perspectives

Theoretical Foundation

Bringing the discoveries of the present study into perspective, the objective of this chapter, is facilitated by the following comment of Schoenberg's from "My Evolution": ". . . in spite of my loosening of the shackles of obsolete aesthetics I did not cease to ask myself for the theoretical foundaton of the freedom of my style."[1] In view of this study's findings, such freedom, as it applies to the harmonic aspect of Op. 19 (and conceivably elsewhere), is aptly described by the term, "loosening," and may be understood to be characterized, not by outright rejection of the major-minor tonal system as has been widely believed, but rather by a substantial loosening or relaxation of traditional constraints. This loosening, this freedom, may be described in terms of (1) retention of certain features of traditional writing, (2) abandonment of others, (3) modification of certain traditional features, and (4) extension of yet others, a description paralleled in Schoenberg's own words by his statement that "most critics of this new style failed to investigate how far the ancient 'eternal' laws of musical aesthetics were *observed* [retention], *spurned* [abandonment], or merely *adjusted* to changed circumstances [modification and/or extension]."[2] (Italics added.)

---

[1] Schoenberg, "My Evolution," in *Style and Idea*, p. 87.

[2] Schoenberg, p. 86.

Presumably the theoretical foundation of the freedom of Schoenberg's atonal style and the theoretical foundation of his atonality itself are one and the same. Clearly the most critical component of this foundation is the harmonic one; hence the present study focuses upon harmony.

In analyzing Op. 19, it is of course well understood that any consideration of aspects of harmony in a single work—however intensive—cannot do more than suggest with reasonable probability what the harmonic component of the foundation might be for the entirety of the composer's atonal corpus. Nevertheless, it is also understood that such a consideration, if in depth, can provide a detailed account of that component as found in the work under investigation, and that this account can serve as a possible model of reference with which to explore harmony in not only the remainder of Schoenberg's atonal music but in that of other composers as well.

The harmonic component of the theoretical foundation of the freedom of Schoenberg's atonal style in Op. 19 is rooted in four basic concepts: (1) organization of pitch with reference to tonal centers; (2) organization of pitch with reference to harmonic roots; (3) the primacy of tertian organization; and (4) background reservoirs. All other features of this component proceed from or rest upon these concepts in keeping with the operations of retention, abandonment, modification, and extension.

Organization with Reference to Tonal Centers

Op 19's organization with reference to tonal centers differs substantially from that usually encountered in traditional tonal works in that the composition as a whole (1) does not have a principal tonal center and (2) is organized rather with reference to a specific succession of centers. This absence, of course, agrees with Schoenberg's own assertion that he had "renounced a tonal center,"[3] while, on the other hand, the existence of a succession of centers—one which includes all of the twelve tones, some of which follow one another very rapidly—corroborates a recent reference to the composer's atonality as "a highly compressed, elusive, yet kaleidoscopic 'tonality' of quickly changing key-centres that embraces the simplest as well as the most complex relationships."[4]

---

[3] Schoenberg, p. 86.

[4] Malcolm MacDonald, *Schoenberg* (London: J. M. Dent and Sons, 1976), p. 90.

As is shown in example 39 above, the Op. 19 succession of tonal centers can readily be formulated as a melodic entity. Because of this readiness, a parallel can be drawn between (1) the composition's organization with reference to this succession and (2) the organization of much traditional music with reference to a cantus firmus. Accordingly, it is thought not unreasonable to regard the succession as a "cantus firmus of tonal centers," to refer to it as such, and to consider the composition's organization of pitch with reference to it as representing an extension of traditional practice. It is of course understood that traditional organization about a cantus firmus was brought about consciously, while organization about a cantus firmus of tonal centers presumably was not.

More important than the succession's capacity to be formulated as a single melodic line, is its inherent readiness to be formulated as the three-voice passage of example 41, above. In view of this readiness, the succession, i.e., the cantus firmus of tonal centers, can be understood as a linear representation, one note at a time, of that passage, in much the same way that an arpeggio can be understood as a linear representation, one note at a time, of a chord.

The three-voice passage is extremely significant in that it shows Op. 19's tonal centers to be organized according to an underlying polyphonic pattern of contours and chords, a pattern in which voice-leading and harmonic vocabulary comply by and large with nineteenth-century practice. This pattern justifies the existence and placement of every tonal center in the composition in terms of the dual role of each in regard to the pattern itself as (1) a member of a contour and (2) a chord tone or non-harmonic tone.

In so justifying each tonal center, the underlying polyphonic pattern affords a meaningful integration of the following within the context of their relationship to itself: (1) the single center of piece II; (2) the five groups of centers of the other five pieces; (3) the order of succession of centers within each group; (4) the order of succession of the single center and of the five groups in regard to each other; and therefore (5) the order of succession of the six pieces themselves within the composition. A basis is thus provided for understanding Op. 19—at least at the background level represented by this pattern—not as an arbitrary collection of marginally related pieces, but rather as an entity itself, a whole consisting of six meaningfully sequenced movements.

Organization of pitch in this work with reference to an underlying polyphonic pattern suggests the Renaissance phenomenon of composition with reference to pre-existent polyphonic materials, a practice encountered in conjunction with the so-called "parody" Mass. Again, it is of course understood that in the case of this type of Mass, such reference was conscious and intentional, whereas in Op. 19 presumably it was not.

Organization with Reference to Harmonic Roots

The broad features of Op. 19's organization with reference to tonal centers find clear counterparts in the work's organization with reference to harmonic roots. Conspicuous examples are the six polyphonic passages suggested by the six successions of harmonic roots (examples 46-51 above). These passages are analogous to the three-voice passage into which the cantus firmus of tonal centers can readily be formulated. They reveal underlying patterns of contours and chords which also comply by and large with nineteenth-century harmonic vocabulary and voice leading. These patterns justify the existence and placement of every root by ascribing to each a dual role as (1) a constituent of a contour and (2) a chord tone or non-harmonic tone. Thus, in all root movements and root shifts within each piece, the roots and intervallic distances involved can be clearly accounted for.

The Primacy of Tertian Organization

Just as the harmonic vocabulary of the polyphonic passages and patterns underlying the deployment of harmonic roots and tonal centers in Op. 19 is founded in tertian practice, so in the Ursatz of piece II and throughout all six of the pieces, chords are either tertian or can be derived from tertian antecedents. In the composition's harmonies themselves, which admit of tertian, dual-membered tertian, diminished-octave tertian, partially quartal, and quartal categorization, and which in size range from monads to thirteenths, not only does the primacy of the tertian principle become evident, but it is as if Schoenberg were in the process of "filling out the tertian system,"[5] bringing it to a point of culmination, and then going well beyond that point.

The vastness of the harmonic variety represented by the above-mentioned chordal categories is such as to contain, and to

---

[5] In the recent translation of the *Harmonielehre* (Arnold Schoenberg, Theory of Harmony, trans. by Roy E. Carter [Berkeley: University of California Press, 1978], p. 399), the composer himself refers to a "filling out [of] the tertian system more or less temporarily" via exploration—as clarified by the translator—of quartal harmony.

provide ample contextual meaning for, seemingly any dissonant interval or combination of dissonant intervals. Accordingly, in this composition *"emancipation of the dissonance"*[6] is a controlled, functional, and natural concomitant of the richness of the harmonic vocabulary.

Statistical evidence of the primacy of tertian organization in Op. 19 is presented in tables 1-3, in the appendix. There, 63.6% of all occurrences of harmonies are listed as tertian (monads through thirteenths), 21.4% as dual-membered tertian (DM fifths through DM thirteenths), 3.5% as diminished-octave tertian, 6.9% as partially quartal, and 4.6% as quartal.[7]

While acknowledging these statistics, it should be understood that tertian primacy in this composition amounts to more than a pronounced majority of tertian, dual-membered tertian, and diminished-octave tertian chordal occurrences. It also means that whenever quartal and partially quartal chords occur, all of which can readily be derived from tertian antecedents, then the actual tertian organization is to be found, not at the surface level, but in the background. The work's best illustration of this situation is offered by piece VI, which, while containing a preponderance of partially quartal harmonies itself, nevertheless derives readily, as do they, from an underlying tertian formulation, as shown in chapter IV (examples 28-33).

The Tonal and Modal Systems: A Structural Reservoir

Because organization of pitch in Op. 19 involves abandonment, modification, and extension of traditional features, as well as their simple retention, the tonal and modal systems, as such, can hardly be regarded as operating continuously at the composition's surface level. Where they do function continuously, however, as may be inferred from the relationship between piece VI and the tertian formulation underlying it, is in the work's background. There, these systems—particularly the tonal

---

[6] Schoenberg, "Composition with Twelve Tones (1)," in *Style and Idea*, pp. 216, 217.

[7] In this study, an "occurrence" of a chord is regarded as an event which commences when the chord begins to sound, continues while the chord sounds or is implied, and ceases when the chord stops sounding or is no longer implied. A chord followed immediately by a larger chord which contains the first (e.g., P.II., mm.1-2: $G:I^3$ followed by $G:I^5$) is not itself regarded as being implied during the occurrence of that larger chord. Individual occurrences vary greatly in duration. Thus, in the succession from $C:I^9$ to $C:I_{\sharp 5}^{9}$ in piece I (m.14), each of these chords occurs but briefly. In contrast, the repeated I^3 at the beginning of piece II has a single prolonged occurrence which ceases only when the ensuing I^5 commences.

one—serve as a vast reservoir of structural relationships, materials, and processes (e.g., tonal functions, tertian chords, and modulation, respectively), doing so as a source of (1) surface-level features of the composition and (2) organizational constraints for the sub-surface structures involved in the underlying relationships described in chapter IV.

1. *Source of Surface-Level Features.* These features come from this reservoir via simple retention, modification, and extension. Important features of the reservoir which in the work's harmonic organization at this level are not present, through any of these three operations, are to be understood as having been abandoned. A summary of surface-level features of this organization, categorized as to retention, modification, extension, and abandonment of features of the reservoir, is offered below:

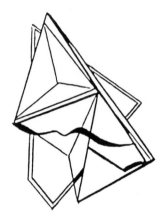

a) *Retention.* Retained features include: (1) tonal centers having local influence; (2) a principal center for piece II (local within the context of Op. 19 as a whole); (3) modulation; (4) major, minor, and Phrygian modal orientations; (5) harmonic roots; (6) tertian harmonies; (7) non-harmonic tones; (8) chord-to-chord movement involving a change of root (the rising perfect fourth being the most frequent interval traversed); (9) conjunct voice-leading; and (10) movement from dissonance to consonance, consonance to dissonance, dissonance to dissonance, and consonance to consonance.

b) *Modification* Modification is observed in: (1) a type of progressive tonality, present in the five modulating pieces and in the composition as a whole, and characterized by often rapid modulation; (2) the conclusion of most cadences in dissonance; (3) octave displacement in otherwise conjunct lines; and (4) frequent obscuration or veiling of traditional tonal functions.

c) *Extension.* Extension of features of the reservoir is represented in that (1) simultaneous major and Phrygian as well as single modal orientations are found, and (2) dual-membered, diminished-octave, partially quartal, and quartal chords occur in addition to tertian harmonies.

d) *Abandonment.* Among features abandoned are: (1) the traditionally expected single principal tonal center for the composition as a whole; (2) a single principal center for each of the five modulating pieces; (3) straightforward traditional cadences; and (4) emphasis on the dominant-tonic relationship.

2. *Source of Constraints for Sub-Surface Structures.*
Organizational constraints for the sub-surface structures described

in chapter IV pertain to matters including primarily: (1) orientation about tonal centers; (2) harmonic vocabulary; (3) harmonic progression; and (4) voice leading. While these constraints come from both the modal and the tonal systems, principally via retention, the influence of the tonal system obtains much more widely than does that of the modal. Thus, for instance, the tonal system provides means of orientation about tonal centers for the six polyphonic passages suggested by the successions of harmonic roots, for the three-voice passage suggested by the cantus firmus of tonal centers, and for the final two-thirds of that cantus. By way of contrast, in these structures the modal system provides the orientation for only the cantus' initial one-third.

Although features of the tonal-modal reservoir transfer to the work's sub-surface structures almost exclusively via retention, rare instances of extension of items from the former's harmonic vocabulary do occur in the latter. One example of such extension is the dual-membered seventh chord ($VII_{\flat 7}^{\natural 7}$) in the four-chord progression derived from the Ursatz of piece II (example 25c, above). Another is the quartal triad ($Q_3 \langle TE \rangle$) found in measures 2 and 3 of the polyphonic passage suggested by piece V's succession of harmonic roots (example 50, above).

Extension is also implied in the organization of the composition with reference to cantus firmus and parody principles. Nevertheless, this organization, strictly speaking, does not represent extension of features of the reservoir, but rather extension of traditional practice associated with that reservoir. Similarly, piece II's demonstrated organization along quasi-Schenkerian lines does not signify extension of features of the reservoir, but extension of the range of applicability of the structure-prolongation concept instead.

The Tonal System: A Reservoir of Expectations

In the above discussion of the role of the tonal and modal systems as a reservoir functioning in the composition's background, the term "background" is used in its general sense. Additionally, however, the findings of the study support an enlightened position advocated by Hans Keller in which this term is given a specialized meaning. The position, stated below, pertains to the role of tonal harmony in regard both to

Schoenberg's atonal and to his serial music. It offers a further
dimension from which to consider the relationship between Op.
19 and the tonal system.

Defining background from a psychological point of view as
"the sum total of well-defined, well-implied and equally well-
suppressed expectations aroused by the composer—well-
suppressed, that is, everywhere except at the very end"[8] (of the
movement or piece), and defining "foreground" as "the sum total
of the composer's meaningful contradictions of his background,"
musical meaning being "the well-defined tension between
foreground and background,"[9] Keller contends that "Schoenberg's
plunge into atonality and its development into dodecaphony
meant the banishment of tonal harmony—not, as he consciously
thought, from his music, but from its foreground into its
background."[10]

If this position is combined with the one just described
concerning the role of the tonal system, then that system can be
understood as not only the principal part of the sub-surface
reservoir of structural relationships, materials, and processes, but
as a reservoir of expectations also, most of which, if aroused in the
course of the composition, will be meaningfully contradicted. The
concept of expectation and its meaningful contradiction is
illustrated below, with two examples from piece III. Then follows
a short list of general categories of contradiction observed in Op.
19.

In the first example (mm. 8-9; see chapter III analysis), the
initial chord of the piece's final cadence is heard as a root-position
dominant-ninth of A♭ major (A♭:V^9). This chord raises an
expectation (background) within the context of the major-minor
tonal system for continued orientation about A♭ as a center, and
for resolution most probably to a root-position tonic triad in that
key. Instead, this expectation is meaningfully contradicted
(foreground) by resolution to a first-inversion tonic triad with
added second in not A♭ major but G minor (g: I$_{a2\ 3}^{\ 5}$).

In the second example (m.1; see chapter III analysis), the
piece's second chord, heard as an inverted tonic ninth of B minor
(b:I$_7^9$), arouses an expectation (background) within the context of
the major-minor tonal system for continued allegiance to B as a
center, probably via further tonic harmony. Meaningful

---

[8] Hans Keller, "Schoenberg's Return to Tonality," *Journal of the Arnold Schoenberg
Institute*, 5 (June 1981), 3.

[9] Keller, p. 4.

[10] Keller, p. 6.

contradiction of this expectation (foreground) occurs as the chord proceeds to tonic harmony in E♭ major rather than in B minor (E♭:I♮7♭7♯5).

General categories of meaningful contradiction of expectation rooted in tonal harmony include: (1) dissonant cadence chords in place of traditionally expected consonant ones; (2) root movement through intervals other than the ascending or descending perfect fourth in cadences ending in tonic harmony; (3) mode mixture in certain passages (e.g., Phrygian and major in piece I); (4) quartal, partially-quartal, and dual-membered chordal structure instead of the traditionally expected tertian harmony; and (5) octave displacement in otherwise conjunct melodic lines.

Atonality and Incomprehensibility

Keller's position and this study's support of it notwithstanding, the prevalence of the view that Op. 19 is atonal in the popular sense of the word suggests the probability that, when hearing this work, many (if not most) listeners experience neither the arousal of expectation nor its meaningful contradiction, that to them the composition's language is simply incomprehensible. Why this should be the case can be explained with reference to the combination of abandonment, modification, and extension of traditional features. Understandably, if no traditional cadences are heard, if the tonic-dominant relationship is not emphasized, if modifications and extensions differ so much from the originals as to be initially (?) unrecognizable, if items which are retained sound strange because they occur within the unfamiliar context of abandoned, modified, and/or extended features, then lack of aural comprehension should hardly be surprising. Further, if chords are but outlined, or if they change mercurially from one to another, and if orientations about tonal centers follow each other with obscuring rapidity, then incomprehension can only be exacerbated. Finally, if for some reason an occasional item or relationship should be recognized and a traditional expectation should be aroused, the contradiction of the latter in a likely unrecognizable fashion may still block any understanding. So, if atonality be equated to current incomprehensibility, as is suggested in Schoenberg's conjecture that "tonal is perhaps nothing more than what is understood *today* and atonal what will be understood in the *future*,"[11] then, for

---

[11] Schoenberg, "Problems of Harmony," in *Style and Idea*, p. 284.

many hearers, this music is for all practical purposes atonal, in the word's popular sense.

However, it does not need to remain that way. As is shown above, Op. 19's harmonic component, certainly this work's most obdurate feature, *can* be explained—*musically*—with reference to the tonal and modal systems out of which the composition's language has developed. Accordingly, aural comprehension of the pieces should be regarded largely as a function of aural and conceptual familiarity with the details and broad characteristics of their harmonic organization. It is hoped that the present study may facilitate acquisition of such familiarity.

Further, it is hoped that the consideration of the *Six Little Piano Pieces* offered herein may make some meaningful contribution towards the creation in due course of a comprehensive theory of harmony in Schoenberg, one which will make conceptual and knowledgeable aural familiarity with the harmonic organization of the composer's pre-serial atonal and twelve-tone music a realizable objective.

Chordal Categories
Relative Frequency of Occurrence

Chordal Category	Number of Occurrences	Total
Tertian (including monads)	110	63.6%
DM Tertian	37	21.4
Dim. 8ve. Tertian	6	3.5
Partially Quartal	12	6.9
Quartal	8	4.6
Total	173	100.0%

Table 2

Chords and Monads - Number of Occurrences

Chord Type or Monad	Piece I	Piece II	Piece III	Piece IV	Piece V	Piece VI	Totals	% Totals
Tertian:								
Monad	0	0	1	1	1	0	3	
3rd	1	7	2	5	1	1	17	
5th	9	2	4 (2 a2, 1 imp)	9 (2 sug)	4	0	28	
7th	9	1	4	1 (1 sug)	9 (3 sug)	4 (all 3rd less)	28	
9th	5	1	6	1	2	0	15	
11th	5	2	2	1	3	0	13	
13th	4	0	0	0	2	0	6	
Total	33	13	19	18	22	5	110	63.6%

Abbreviations:

a2   means "with an added second"

sug   means "suggested"

imp   means "implied"

Table 2 - continued

Chord Type or Monad	Piece I	Piece II	Piece III	Piece IV	Piece V	Piece VI	Totals	% Totals
DM Tertian:								
5th	6	0	4	0	1	0	11	
7th	6 (1 imp)	1	2	2	2	0	13	
9th	1	0	0	1	3 (1 sug)	0	5	
11th	4	0	0	1	0	0	5	
13th	1	1	0	0	0	1	3	
Total	18	2	6	4	6	1	37	21.4%
Dim. 8ve. Tertian:								
7d8	1	0	0	0	1	0	2	
9d8	1	0	0	1	1 (imp)	0	3	
11d8	1	0	0	0	0	0	1	
Total	3	0	0	1	2	0	6	3.5%
Partially Quartal:								
$PQ\langle 13\rangle$	1	0	1	0	0	1	3	
$PQ\langle DM\,11\rangle$	0	0	0	0	0	6	6	
$PQ\langle DM\,13\rangle$	0	0	1	0	0	2	3	
Total	1	0	2	0	0	9	12	6.9%
Quartal:								
$Q_3\langle TE\rangle$	2	0	0	1	0	0	3	
$Q_4\langle 11\rangle$	1	0	2	0	0	1	4	
$Q_6\langle 11\rangle$	0	0	0	1	0	0	1	
Total	3	0	2	2	0	1	8	4.6%
Totals	58	15	29	25	30	16	173	100.0%

Table 3

Chords and Monads - Relative Frequency of Occurrence [1]

Prevalence Ranking	Chord Type or Monad	Number of Occurrences	% of Total
1	5th chord	28	16.2%
	7th	28	16.2
2	3rd	17	9.8
3	9th	15	8.7
4	11th	13	7.5
	DM 7th	13	7.5
5	DM 5th	11	6.4
6	13th	6	3.5
	$PQ\langle DM\ 11\rangle$	6	3.5
7	DM 9th	5	2.9
	DM 11th	5	2.9
8	$Q_4\langle 11\rangle$	4	2.3
9	Monad	3	1.7
	DM 13th	3	1.7
	9d8	3	1.7
	$PQ\langle 13\rangle$	3	1.7
	$PQ\langle DM\ 13\rangle$	3	1.7
	$Q_3\langle TE\rangle$	3	1.7
10	7d8	2	1.2
11	11d8	1	0.6
	$Q_6\langle 11\rangle$	1	0.6
Total		173	100.0%

---

[1] The term "occurrence is defined in footnote 5 of chapter V.

Table 4

Root Movements and Shifts[2]

Relative Frequency of Occurrence

	Interval	Number of Occurrences	% of Total
Root	P4 ↑ (P5↓)	18	14.5%
Movements	P4 ↓ (P5↑)	14	11.3
	m2 ↑	13	10.5
	M3 ↓	13	10.5
	m3 ↓	12	9.7
	M3 ↑	8	6.5
	m2 ↓	7	5.6
	tt ↕	7	5.6
	M2 ↑	5	4.0
	A1 ↑	4	3.2
	M2 ↓	3	2.4
	m3 ↑	3	2.4
	d4 ↓	3	2.4
	d3 ↑	2	1.6
	A2 ↓	2	1.6
	d4 ↑	2	1.6
Total		116	93.4%
Root	d3 ↓	3	2.4
Shifts	A1 ↓	1	0.8
	d3 ↑	1	0.8
	m3 ↓	1	0.8
	A3 ↑	1	0.8
	dd5 ↑	1	0.8
Total		8	6.4%
Total		124	99.8%

---

[2] All changes of root listed here take place within and not between pieces.

Bibliography

Bradshaw, Merrill K. "Tonal Structure in the Early Works of Anton Webern." D.Mus.A. thesis. University of Illinois, 1962. 159 p. (Xerox. Microfilm. Ann Arbor, Michigan: Xerox University Microfilms. Order No. 62-6106).

Hicken, Kenneth L. "Schoenberg's 'Atonality': Fused Bitonality?" *Tempo*, 109 (June 1974), 27-36.

_____."Structure and Prolongation: Tonal and Serial Organization in the 'Introduction' of Schoenberg's *Variations for Orchestra*." Ph.d. dissertation. Brigham Young University, 1970. 192 p. (Xerox. Microfilm. Ann Arbor, Michigan: Xerox University Microfilms. Order No. 71-8856).

_____."Structure and Prolongation: Tonal and Serial Organization in the 'Introduction' of Schoenberg's Variations for Orchestra" (summary of author's Ph.D. dissertation), *Musicological Annual*, 10 (Ljubljana, Yugoslavia: 1974), 27-47.

_____."Tonal Organization in Schoenberg's *Six Little Piano Pieces*, Op. 19," *Canadian University Music Review*, 1 (1980), 130-146.

_____."Towards a Theory of Harmony in Schoenberg's Twelve-Tone Music," in *Bericht über den 1. Kongress der Internationalen Schönberg-Gesellschaft* (1974). Edited by Rudolf Stephan. Vienna: Elisabeth Láfite, 1978. (Pages 87-97.)

Keller, Hans. "Schoenberg's Return to Tonality," *Journal of the Arnold Schoenberg Institute*, 5 (June 1981), 2-21.

MacDonald, Malcolm. *Schoenberg*. The Master Musicians Series. London: J. M. Dent and Sons, 1976. xiv, 289 p.

Schoenberg, Arnold. *Sechs kleine Klavierstücke*, Op. 19. [Vienna]: Universal Edition, c1913, copyright renewed 1940 by Arnold Schoenberg. 8 p.

_____. *Style and Idea: Selected Writings of Arnold Schoenberg*. Edited by Leonard Stein. Translations by Leo Black. New York: St. Martins Press, 1975. 559 p.

_____. *Theory of Harmony*. Translated by Roy E. Carter. Berkeley: University of California Press, 1978. xxii, 441 p.